The Light Giver

A HELPFUL RESOURCE FOR SOCIAL EMOTIONAL LEARNING

The Light Giver

and Other Stories to Raise Emotionally Healthy Children

PEGGY D. SIDERATOS
Illustrated by Stamatia Mavrikos

For the Love of Children Press
Brooklyn, New York

Copyright © 2019 by Peggy D. Sideratos

Published by For the Love of Children Press

Brooklyn, New York, 11209

All rights reserved.

This book may not be reproduced in whole or in part without written permission from the publisher, except by a reviewer who may quote brief passages in a review; nor may any part of this book be reproduced, stored in a retrieval system, or transmitted in any form or by any means, electronic, mechanical, photocopying, recording or other, without written permission from the publisher.

For the Love of Children Press

The Lightgiver ISBN (Hardcover): 978-1-7334620-0-6

The Lightgiver ISBN (Paperback): 978-1-7334620-2-0

The Lightgiver Stories Workbook ISBN: 978-1-7334620-1-3

Editing by Red Letter Editing, www.redletterediting.com

Cover and interior illustrations by Stamatia Mavrikos

Cover and interior design and layout by Constellation Books Services

Acknowledgments

No man walks this path alone. I want to thank God, Jesus, and Archangel Gabriel for the inspiration, guidance, wisdom, and grace to create this program. I also want to thank my mom, Despina, and my late father, Demetrios, who have always been my greatest teachers, my biggest supporters, and the most beautiful parents in the world. Thank you for your unwavering love and devotion; it has been my greatest source of strength. My love, respect, and admiration for you grows exponentially with each passing year.

I want to thank my extraordinary brother, Steven. You have always gone out of your way to help and support me and have especially done so for this project. You are brilliant, kind, and compassionate, and I am incredibly blessed to have you in my life. You are my best friend, my confidant, and my hero.

Thank you also, to my "sisters" Peggy and Eleni, who have always been so supportive and loving. You two are among the most beautiful souls I have ever known, and have brought such beauty into my life. I love and adore you. Peggy, thank you for your amazing guidance and insights on my stories and lessons, and for encouraging me so many times when I felt completely overwhelmed.

Thank you, Stamatia, for bringing my stories to life with your beautiful artwork and for all the love and attention you poured into your work. I enjoyed working with you so much and marvel at your talent and the kindness of your heart. Thank you, Markella, for helping me get set up for this venture and for the priceless gift of your friendship.

Thank you to my godson, Hercules, for creating my website and being so patient with me. You are an amazing young man and I am so proud to be your godmother. Thank you, Maria Elena, for all your valuable input. Your passion and love for others and your strength inspire me.

Thank you to Martha Bullen and all the staff members of Quantum Leap for guiding me on this journey and showing me the way. Thank you, Jessica and Christy, for your hard work preparing my manuscripts for publication. Thank you also to my extended family, koumbari, and friends, who always encouraged me to "go for it." You make my life so much richer.

To my amazing and beautiful godchildren, all my cousins' children, my former students, and to all the Dafnonas youth, thank you for always teaching me so much, and for continually filling my heart with such joy.

Thank you, Joyce Meyer, for your exceptional wisdom and guidance, which enabled me to heal. Thank you, Junior, for filling a broken piece of my heart with so much love, sweet snuggles, and wet kisses.

And to my dear friend Michael, who left this world too soon. Your light has left a lasting impression on the hearts of so many of us. We love and miss you.

Contents

Introduction	1
Part I: Facing Discouragement and Encouraging Others	**5**
1. The Light Giver	7
2. Gabriel's Journey	15
3. The Messenger	21
Part II: Handling Criticism and Negativity	**27**
4. The Most Beautiful Girl in the World	29
5. It's Your Choice	35
6. The Big, Ugly, Heavy Suitcase	41
Part III: Dealing with Guilt	**49**
7. The Race	51
8. The Guilt Bugs	59
Part IV: Facing Fear	**65**
9. The What-If Monster	67
10. Do It Afraid	73
11. The Truth Behind Their Words	79
Part V: Being Your Best and Not Comparing Yourself to Others	**87**
12. Let Your Light Shine	89
13. Not Like Everybody Else	95
14. Being a Person of Excellence	101

Part VI: Coping with Disappointment, Envy, and Preconceived Views   107

     15. Eleni's Disappointment   109

     16. Tommy's Bike   117

     17. Tuning In to Your Truth   125

Part VII: Kindness and Compassion   133

     18. Penny's Surprise   135

     19. A Trip to the Senior Home   143

     20. A Double Test of Patience   151

Part VIII: The True Meaning of Love   159

     21. Love Is a Way to Live   161

     22. There's Always Room for More   167

Story Directory   175

Introduction

The majority of people, despite differences in culture, religion, or social or economic background, are fundamentally similar at their core. At the heart of every human being is a desire to live a good and happy life. We yearn to be loved, to be valued, to connect with others, and to feel good about ourselves.

In theory it sounds so simple, and yet at times it is these simple things that seem to elude us. The truth is, we live in a world that, despite its modern-day conveniences, has become complicated and full of emotional stress. While insecurity, anxiety, and fears have always been a part of our human experience, it seems that people are struggling with pain and suffering more than ever before. This is especially true of our children. We live in a world today where kids and teens are dealing with depression, anxiety, cutting, eating disorders, bullying, school shootings, and suicide rates at an alarming level. The brokenness is escalating. Our children are hurting, and we have to do something about it.

My experience as an educator in the classroom helped me realize early on the importance of addressing issues of self-esteem and good character with my students. I quickly noticed that when kids had more self-confidence and felt better about their place in the world, their academic performance was better, the relationships between themselves and others was healthier, and most importantly, there was an inner contentment that shone through.

My findings have been validated by numerous studies on Social Emotional Learning (SEL). SEL instruction teaches children how to regulate emotions, improve communication skills, foster empathy, build confidence, and make better decisions. More schools are now implementing SEL into their curriculums because of the numerous benefits it brings, including positive effects on behavior issues and increases in student academic achievement. Research has also shown long-term benefits that follow children into adulthood. Children with SEL instruction are less likely to be involved in criminal activity and substance abuse, and suffer from fewer mental health issues.

During my more than fourteen years of teaching, finding materials to support my efforts to address these social emotional needs in my students was often difficult. It was increasingly harder for parents who had even less exposure to educational materials. Like many other teachers and parents already inundated with pressures of meeting children's other needs, I didn't always have the time or energy to invest in tracking down such materials. As a result, I decided to create a collection of stories and lessons to address a volume of social emotional topics for children that would be easy for anyone to use and wouldn't require a huge investment of time.

My experience with children taught me that one of the most effective ways to communicate and relate to them is through storytelling. Children are always engaged during story time, and especially so when we discuss how we can personally relate to the characters, so I decided to use this strategy to create my program.

The Light Giver and Other Stories to Raise Emotionally Healthy Children is a helpful resource to address a variety of social and emotional skills through storytelling and shared experiences. Each story addresses a single core value or life lesson and touches on others. The stories can be read to and enjoyed by children as young as five and up to age twelve. On average the stories are written at approximately a fourth-grade independent reading level. The majority of them center on children and address difficulties and real-life challenges they face. Discussion questions and a helpful list of vocabulary words are found at the end of each story. I intentionally included challenging vocabulary as I believe it is important to expose children to as many new words as possible. The lists were included to serve as an additional resource to teachers and parents.

The stories are grouped by a variety of general topics such as facing discouragement, fear, disappointment, and envy, and give children coping skills to deal with these emotions. Some stories stress the importance of patience, kindness, compassion, and striving to become their personal best without expecting perfection or comparing themselves to others. Some teach about the personal fulfillment that comes by helping people. The stories also touch on other tenets of good character, such as respect, patience, honesty, and integrity, and how these traits affect the individual and others. Finally, they teach that love is not merely a feeling but a decision made daily about how to treat people.

For a brief summary of each story and a description of the issues they address, please refer to the Story Directory at the back of the book. I have also published a separate resource of lessons and corresponding discussions that elaborate on the topics found in each story in a separate supplement, *The Light Giver Stories Workbook*. While the lessons in this resource are designed to complement each story, each lesson can stand alone and be used without having read the story beforehand. The lessons and activities can be utilized by parents with their own children, in small group settings by youth counselors, and in classroom settings. The book is available for purchase from a variety of vendors. For additional information on the book and the lessons it includes, please visit my website at www.thelightgiverstories.com.

It is my sincere hope and intention that these stories help foster communication lines between children and adults and prove to be an enjoyable and valuable way for them to connect with each other and learn. There is no replacement for good parenting, and this collection is not meant to be a magic remedy to address all the challenges parents face. However, the stories can definitely help spark indispensable conversations and result in closer relationships between adults and children, subsequently helping to nourish each child's soul. This collection of stories was a labor of love, all for the love of children.

PART I
Facing Discouragement and Encouraging Others

STORY ONE
The Light Giver

There he was, having lunch with someone at the local diner. I had heard about him from quite a few people in town, as if he were a local celebrity, but I hadn't imagined what he looked like. I realized who he was only after I heard someone tell the waiter, "I want to pay the lunch check for the Light Giver and his friend over there."

My curiosity piqued, I couldn't help but look over at him. He was an average-looking man, not especially tall or big in size, nor especially handsome, but I did see a kindness in his eyes as he smiled and shared a laugh with the man next to him. I was glad to have the opportunity to see him myself because, despite my being in town for just a few weeks, I had heard several people mention him. I didn't remember his real name, but I knew that people referred to him by his nickname, the Light Giver.

When someone first told me his nickname, I asked if he was a religious leader, a local politician, or some sort of scholar, but I was told Mike wasn't any of those things; he was simply a middle-aged man who worked in carpentry and labored most of the day, just like everyone else. He had been in town for ten years, and during that time he had built a reputation among the townspeople as a person who always had an ear to listen and good advice to share. Mike had the natural ability of knowing just what to say to make people feel better about whatever situation they were facing. He never claimed to have all the answers, but the

8 FACING DISCOURAGEMENT AND ENCOURAGING OTHERS

insight he shared with them always gave them a sense of comfort. What people loved about him most of all, though, was his humility and grace. He freely shared whatever wisdom he had with others and never asked for anything in return, which earned him the love and respect of many.

The first time I heard of the Light Giver was the day I arrived to town. A gentleman had come by the house I had rented for the month to drop off my rental car. He had asked me why I had chosen to visit the town, as it was not a typical vacation destination. I explained that I was a novelist and needed a quiet place to get some inspiration and begin writing my next book. He suggested I speak with the Light Giver, because he always seemed to know how to help others.

My visitor had said, "Five years ago, when I was unhappy at my old job, he encouraged me to open my own business. He asked me what I would do if I could magically take away all the fear thoughts from my head, and I told him I would open my own rental car company. Mike told me to make my plans and move toward that direction, and to leave the fear by the wayside. It took me two years to get my company going, but I've never been happier."

"That was some really good advice," I said. "It's been a great help to me that you opened your business, because there aren't any other rental car companies nearby."

I thanked him for bringing the car and went back inside to unpack my things and get settled. I didn't give the suggestion of talking to the Light Giver a second thought, as I was all wrapped up in my own thoughts of my book.

I spent the next two days by myself in the rental house trying to create an interesting story, but it wasn't working. I was unhappy with everything I thought of, and I knew that if I wasn't passionate about what I was writing, my readers would feel that, too. I took a walk to explore my new surroundings, hoping the change in scenery would spark my creative juices.

After walking for a while, I came across a bakery and decided to stop inside. The smell of the fresh cinnamon rolls was intoxicating, so I indulged in one, along with a cup of coffee, and sat down to enjoy it. At the table next to me sat an elderly couple, who began to chat with me about the delicious cinnamon rolls. They asked me if I was new in town or just visiting, and I told them about the house I had rented for a short stay.

I learned that Tom and Edna had lived in the town all their lives and had been married for fifty-three years. Since they seemed to know everyone, I asked if they could recommend somebody to repair the garage door. The electronic door opener was working for the first couple of days after I had arrived but wasn't anymore. They suggested I give the Light Giver a call.

"I keep hearing about him. Who is this guy, and why on earth does everybody call him the Light Giver?" I asked.

"Oh, that's the nickname we gave Mike right after he moved to town because he updated all the electrical fixtures in our home," Edna said. "He fixed the lights, so we called him the Light Giver. Then people started using the name because not only did he know how to fix almost anything in your house, but he also had a knack for knowing how to bring light into people's situations. He's full of great advice and insight, and he's so funny, which helps cheer people up when they are feeling down. The metaphor worked, and the nickname stuck. Mike just laughs it off, though."

Now here he was, seated next to me in the diner. I finally had the chance to meet the Light Giver face-to-face and find out if what everybody was saying about him was true. I stuck out my hand and introduced myself.

"Hi, I'm Steve. Are you the Light Giver? I was told you might be able to fix my garage door."

He shrugged and said, "Yes, I can help you, but please just call me Mike." He agreed to stop by the next day to take a look at the door and try to fix it.

I was intrigued by his reputation, so when he came the next day, I was surprised at how normal he was. He wasn't spewing words of wisdom or anything deeply philosophical. We talked about the garage door, and he asked me about my career—nothing out of the ordinary. He told me he had to order a part for the door and would be back in two days. After he left, I wondered if the name people had labeled him with made him uncomfortable, as it may set high expectations about him. I wondered if it stressed him at all. I decided to ask him about it when he came back later that week.

The day was unusually cold when Mike came back two days later, so I asked him if he wanted to join me for a cup of coffee before he began. He readily accepted. We sat with our palms wrapped around the hot coffee mugs, and in keeping with polite conversation, he asked me how my writing was going. I told him I was experiencing writer's block and that it was beginning to stress me. Then I asked him whether or not it bothered him or put any pressure on him when people called him the Light Giver.

"I really don't pay that much attention to the name," he said. "It's nice to have people appreciate my help, but the moment people give more attention to a label, the less that person is able to truly help. I've seen this happen to people all the time. They get a job title or hit a level of success, and then they want to keep it up or not disappoint others with their next project. They lose sight of the joy and fun that sharing their gift with others can bring. The pressure of living up to the job title or the responsibility takes all the fun away."

His response struck a chord with me because I realized I had fallen into the same pattern. I was disappointed with myself because I had produced neither the quality nor the quantity of writing that I thought I should have. The more pressure I put on myself, the more blocked I became.

While I didn't reveal my sudden revelation to him at that moment, I had to ask, "What advice do you give people when that happens?"

He said, "I tell them what my mom always told me. When you can't help yourself, help somebody else." I thought that was a strange answer but just shook my head.

Mike fixed the door in a matter of minutes and was on his way. I didn't think he was much of a light giver, but he sure was good at his work.

The next morning, as I stared at my computer screen waiting for a brilliant idea to pop into my head for my novel, I couldn't help but think of Mike's words. "When you can't help yourself, help somebody else." Maybe I should give that a try. I knew Tom and Edna were having a garage sale that day, so I decided to go by and offer to help. The morning after that, I went to the bakery and offered to deliver some baked goods to the soup kitchen, and while I was there, I volunteered to help serve food for a few hours. The following day, I helped my neighbor carry in her groceries and offered to help her son with his homework. I didn't do any writing at all, but I felt great. I took the pressure off myself and experienced joy again—and then it hit me. I got an idea for my novel, and when I sat down to write, it started to pour out of me.

I wrote for two whole days, then decided to get a meal at the diner. There, sitting in the booth where I first met him, was the Light Giver. I went over to express my gratitude to him for the advice he gave me, and told him how it helped inspire me to begin my new novel.

"Now I know why they call you the Light Giver," I said. "Your wisdom is a light that helps others see their way through difficulty."

He looked at me with a small grin and said, "We are all light givers. Within each of us are gifts and wisdom, kindness and compassion, and patience and love to share. Sometimes when we're sad or down or under pressure, we start to believe that the light within us has dimmed. We start focusing on our fears and worries and stop listening to our inner voice. We just need to let go of the fear and pressure we put on ourselves and focus on others. That's when we get clarity, and then our light can shine brighter than the sun."

I never forgot that piece of advice. Whenever I start to feel downhearted, stressed, or have to make an important decision and don't know what to do, I always reach out to help somebody else. When I stop focusing on myself, clarity always comes.

I heard that the Light Giver passed away just a year after my stay in the little town. I was shocked to hear about his unexpected passing, as he was relatively young. I heard that people held candles at his funeral to honor some of the light he had brought into their lives. I was overseas at the time promoting my novel, which I dedicated to him. The inscription read, "This book is dedicated to my dear friend the Light Giver, who reminded me that we are all just a reflection of the light we share with one another."

Helpful Vocabulary Words and Discussion Questions for "The Light Giver"

Vocabulary words: destination, politician, pique, refer, carpentry, reputation, humility, grace, passionate, fixtures, insight, metaphor, intrigued, philosophical, spew, expectations, revelation, clarity, inscription, chord

Discussion Questions

1. If you have ever had difficulty trying to start a new project or write a story, how did you handle it?

2. What do you think Mike meant when he said, "We are all light givers"?

3. What is some of the best advice you have ever received? How did it prove to be valuable?

STORY TWO
Gabriel's Journey

Gabriel could hear the sounds of laughter from the children running and playing outside, and he wondered if he would ever be able to run again. It had been three difficult and painful months since the accident that had left him in a wheelchair. He had been released from the hospital only a couple of weeks before, but he was still enduring hours of painful physical therapy daily. The day he came home from the hospital, he had seen his bike standing by the garage door, waiting for him like an old friend. This was a difficult time for him, as he had previously been so active.

Gabriel had never been one to complain much before, but his patience was wearing thin. Although his doctors and parents told him to never give up the hope of walking again, all he could feel now was anger and frustration. The doctors had hoped his body would have responded to the physical therapy more rapidly, but his body was not cooperating the way it used to, the way he wanted it to. Everyone was trying to stay positive and encourage him as much as possible, but he had overheard conversations between his parents and the doctors, who said that they weren't sure he would walk again, despite his having some feeling in his legs. He could see the worry conveyed in his parents' faces and how their eyes occasionally filled with tears, despite trying to hide them.

Gabriel was facing a future of uncertainty, and this made him very uncomfortable. Unlike many ten-year-olds, who consistently change their minds about what they want to be when they grow up, Gabriel had a definite plan: he wanted to be a pilot. In fact, from the time he was a toddler he had been fascinated by planes and the process by which they flew. Although he had been on an airplane only twice in his life, on one of those occasions he had been given the opportunity to visit the cockpit after the plane had landed. His uncle worked for an airline and had set up the visit for him. Visiting the cockpit had intensified Gabriel's desire to become a pilot. Now he sat in his room wondering if that dream would ever become a reality.

At seven o'clock the next morning, his parents came into his room to help him get ready for his daily visit to the rehabilitation center where he did his physical therapy. Getting in and out of the wheelchair was still challenging for him, as was getting into the car. Gabriel's parents were always patient and helpful, but his anger and frustration about his handicap kept growing. He felt defeated by his condition, and after only ten minutes of that day's painful physical therapy, he hit his breaking point.

"I hate this!" he screamed. "It's not working, and I'll never be able to walk! None of you understand what this is like or how painful it is! You just keep telling me to be patient and keep trying. Well, I've been trying, and I still can't walk! I hate that I can't just get up and go to the bathroom or get things off the top shelf or ride my bike. I need help to do everything now! Leave me alone. I don't want to do this anymore! My life is ruined. I'll never be able to do everything I want to, and I'll never be a pilot!" A waterfall of tears cascaded down his cheeks.

His parents tried to console him, and his physical therapist told him they would take a break for him to relax. After a few minutes and some tears shed, he felt slightly better but was still frustrated and angry. Then he noticed an adorable little girl with the biggest brown eyes and the cutest pigtails, who couldn't have been older than six, coming toward him. Her face displayed the kindest smile, and when she came closer he realized that a pair of prosthetic leg braces were attached at her mid-thighs; she was missing her lower legs. She took hold of his hand and squeezed it tightly. She didn't introduce herself but just stood for a minute, holding his hand. Finally she said, "It's all right. Everything will get better."

Gabriel was stunned, not only by this little girl's kindness but by the strength she demonstrated and was trying to bestow on him. He mustered a "thanks," and the little girl smiled again, revealing a gap where one of her baby teeth was missing. Although she was so young, her bravery and compassion were beyond her years. When she let go of Gabriel's hand and slowly walked away, he saw the limp that accompanied her stride.

Gabriel unexpectedly found he was no longer focused on his recovery and limitations but on hers. When his physical therapist came back to work with him, he no longer complained of his discomfort or wallowed in self-pity. All he could think of was that adorable, gapped-tooth little girl.

The next time he came in for his session, he looked for the little girl, but she wasn't around. He had found out that her name was Tabitha, but he never saw her again, as her family had decided to take her to another facility that was closer to their home.

That brief encounter with Tabitha had made a lasting impression on Gabriel. From then on, during the remainder of his recovery, whenever he was physically exhausted or frustrated with his progress, he would think of that beautiful little girl and her words, and it would motivate him and give him newfound strength.

Gabriel's recovery was a long journey, filled with many obstacles and many wonderful highlights. After he graduated, he worked for a company that designs planes. A few years later, he felt compelled to study about prosthetics and is now heavily involved in that field. Although he never became a professional pilot, he did get his pilot's license and now flies small private planes as a hobby.

While he never did learn what became of Tabitha, he has wondered many times how her life is going. He has never forgotten the moment she appeared before him and the lasting effect she has had on his life. Now, by helping to improve the lives of others who need prosthetics, Gabriel feels he can repay the gift that this little girl had bestowed on him.

One truly never knows just how great an impact one small gesture of compassion can have on another.

Helpful Vocabulary Words and Discussion Questions for "Gabriel's Journey"

Vocabulary words: endure, frustration, definite, convey, fascinated, rehabilitation, prosthetic, stunned, bestow, limitations, wallow, discomfort, facility, encounter, motivate, gesture, defeated, uncertain, daily, waterfall

Discussion Questions

1. Why did Tabitha's words and actions have such a profound effect on Gabriel?

2. If you have ever been frustrated by a challenge and wanted to give up, how did you handle it?

3. If anyone has ever offered you words of encouragement, what did they do or say that was helpful? If you have ever encouraged a friend or loved one, how did it make you feel?

STORY 3
The Messenger

Gateway had always been an average, ordinary town until one summer, when it all turned upside-down. I remember that summer so well. I was a young reporter who had just signed on to work for *The Gateway Herald* when my editor asked me to cover my first story. Apparently, Mr. Fredo, a local firefighter, had received a mysterious letter that morning, with no return address or postage. "What's the big deal about that?" you may ask. That's exactly the reaction I had that morning when my editor told me about it. "I heard the contents of this letter are very unusual, Jack, so go check it out," she said.

It didn't take me long to get to the Fredo residence, and when I arrived, a few of Mr. Fredo's friends were standing outside of his house with him.

"What's the big deal about the letter you received, Mr. Fredo?" I asked.

He said, "It's the oddest thing. I have no idea who sent it, as it is signed 'The Messenger.' There is no postage or return address on it. None of us here recognize the handwriting, either. The sender must have slipped it under my door during the night."

"Well, what does it say?" I asked, still wondering what the big fuss was about.

Mr. Fredo read, "I know you have a secret talent that you are afraid to share with the world. Don't let that gift go to waste. When you share your gifts with the world, you spread joy and make the world more beautiful. —The Messenger."

"Well, what's your secret talent?" I asked. "One of your friends must know about it and wants you to use it. I don't know why they would want to remain anonymous, but maybe they are hesitant to tell you face-to-face." Mr. Fredo's puzzled expression piqued my curiosity even more.

"Well," he replied, "I can play the violin, but I haven't played in years. In fact, my violin has been in my attic since I moved here fifteen years ago. I haven't thought about it in a very long time. None of my friends here even know I used to play."

I shrugged and said, "Well somebody must have found out, and they want you to start again."

Later, I checked in with my editor and told her about the letter from The Messenger. I said I didn't think it was anything worth writing about or investigating. That changed, though, the very next day.

The newspaper got a call about a second letter from The Messenger, but this time the letter was sent to Ms. Pickerson, a nurse at the local high school. As with Mr. Fredo's letter, there was no postage or return address. When I met with Ms. Pickerson at her apartment, she read me the letter. "I know there is something on your mind that is troubling you, but have faith. Things always have a way of working out in the end. —The Messenger."

She looked at me and said, "Can you please try to find out who sent this to me? I haven't discussed this with anyone yet, but I'm considering moving back home to Ohio to care for my aging parents. I have not told a soul about this, not my friends or my colleagues, not even my parents. How could anyone possibly know?"

"I don't have an answer for you," I told her. "Maybe one of your friends thought you looked preoccupied lately and sent it."

"Well, none of my friends have admitted to sending it to me, and I don't recognize the handwriting."

"Funny, that's what Mr. Fredo said yesterday," I said.

"Who's Mr. Fredo? Did he receive a note from The Messenger?" Ms. Pickerson asked.

"Yes, he did, and I think I'm seeing the beginning of a very interesting story starting to develop."

Now the mysterious letters were compelling me to investigate this further. I tried but couldn't find any link between the two recipients. The next morning, as I was typing up my story about the mystery messenger, my editor called me into her office.

"Jack, there's a third letter," she said. "This recipient is a twelve-year-old named Molly Peterson. Go find out what the letter says before you write another word."

When I interviewed Molly and her parents, I found out that they had moved to Gateway a few weeks before and didn't know many people in town. Neither Molly nor her parents had ever met Mr. Fredo or Ms. Pickerson, and like them, they didn't recognize the handwriting in the letter. I noticed that it was the same handwriting as in the other two letters.

Molly read the letter. "You are more beautiful and special than you know. Your inner beauty radiates wherever you go. —The Messenger." As she read it to

24 FACING DISCOURAGEMENT AND ENCOURAGING OTHERS

me, I saw her eyes light up and a bright smile surface, as if these were the exact words she needed to hear at this moment in her life. "I can see that those words really touch you," I said.

I was completely stumped; I had no clue how to solve this mystery. When I wrote my article, I asked the townspeople to help me figure it out.

The next day yet another letter surfaced, and the entire town was talking about it. This one was addressed to Mr. Handler, the butcher at Parson's Meat Market. He read the letter out loud. "Don't ever let fear make your decisions for you. Trust your instinct and your heart. —The Messenger." After he read it, he started laughing. "I read about The Messenger, but I never thought I'd get one of these letters. I think I needed to hear this. I have really enjoyed working at and managing Parson's Meat Market for the past fifteen years. Now Mr. Parson wants to retire, and he has offered to sell me the business. I really want to buy the store, but I've been afraid of making the commitment. This note reminds me to not let my fear get in the way of my dream. I guess I owe The Messenger a thank you." I smiled and told Mr. Handler that I would express his appreciation to The Messenger in my next article, which I did.

The notes from The Messenger continued daily for three months and led to interactions between the townspeople. The newspaper started receiving letters from our readers who, while not recipients of the notes, were so moved by them that they were writing their own encouraging notes to others, sometimes anonymously and sometimes not. We even heard about people in two neighboring towns who started to do the same.

Eventually The Messenger retired, but beautiful messages from others continued to be shared long afterward. People were moved to send inspirational messages to hospitals, retirement homes, and military members overseas. I was glad I had been chosen to report the story, but it bothered me that I couldn't ever figure out the identity of The Messenger.

At the end of the year, I wrote a follow-up story about the effect The Messenger had had on the people of our town and beyond. The day after I submitted the story, I was surprised to find myself the recipient of a note from The Messenger. It read, "You inspire others with your work and make a difference in the world. —The Messenger" I chuckled to myself and thought, "So do you, my dear Messenger, so do you."

Helpful Vocabulary Words and Discussion Questions for "The Messenger"

Vocabulary words: contents, fuss, anonymous, investigate, recipient, radiate, stumped, instinct, interaction, among, commitment, inspirational, chuckle, submit, colleague, preoccupied, retirement, hesitant, editor, local

Discussion Questions

1. Why do you think The Messenger wished to remain anonymous?
2. How do you suppose The Messenger knew what to write to each of the recipients?
3. Why do you think others started sending inspirational messages?

PART II
Handling Criticism and Negativity

STORY 4
The Most Beautiful Girl in the World

> "WORDS ARE POWERFUL"

Erica was a young girl who was her parents' pride and joy. She was adorable, with eyes as blue as the Mediterranean Sea and long, curly brown hair that cascaded around her shoulders. She always had a smile on her face, and her warm, bubbly personality was infectious.

Erica enjoyed playing with her friends and cousins and spending time with her parents. When her dad came home from a hard day's work, he would swoop her up in his arms and tell her, "You're the most beautiful girl in the world." And she believed him, for she had no reason not to. Her parents were the smartest and kindest people she knew, and the love they showed her was at the root of her happy nature.

Erica started school when she turned five, and her happy days continued. She was lucky enough to have one of her cousins and her best friend in her class, so she spent a lot of time with them. Erica really loved school, but she was not a big fan of homework. Every afternoon, she and her mom would sit at the counter in her mom's clothing store, where she would do her homework. She enjoyed doing it there because many of her mom's customers were friendly, and some would occasionally offer to help her. Her mom would joke with her and say, "I think my customers keep coming back just to spend time with you. You're good for my business."

When Erica was ten years old, her mom sold the clothing store, and she and her family moved into a lovely new home. Although Erica no longer saw her mom's friendly customers, she enjoyed being home with her mom and made new friends in the neighborhood. She was still a very happy girl. Her dad no longer swooped her up in his arms, but day after day he would hug her as soon as he walked through the door and say, "You're the most beautiful girl in the world." And she believed him, for she had no reason to doubt him. He was still the smartest and kindest man she knew, and hearing him say that still made her feel special and loved.

Erica's school life changed dramatically the following year. Although she still had the same classmates, whom she had known for years, they began teasing her. They made fun of her hair, which was now shorter, thicker, and more unruly. It frizzed up in the rain, and no matter how much she tried, she couldn't control and style it the way she wanted.

The teasing began with one mean comment by a girl, but soon a few of the boys joined in, perhaps because they thought it was funny or they were trying to be cool and impress the girls they had crushes on.

Erica couldn't understand why her classmates were suddenly so cruel to her, and her joy and confidence began to deteriorate. At the end of the year, one of the boys in her class wrote in her yearbook, "I killed my dog because it looked like you." Reading it crushed her spirit. Although her friends and cousins tried to get the kids to stop picking on her, the teasing continued throughout the next year.

Erica didn't like to talk about the teasing because it just made her feel worse, so she kept quiet about the bullying and never mentioned it to her parents or teachers. Her parents didn't know how much she was hurting inside. When her dad would come home, he would still hug her and say, "You're the most beautiful girl in the world," but now she no longer believed him. She would say, "You're just saying that because you're my dad," but he would insist that he was saying it because it was true. She wouldn't argue with him about it because it was still nice to hear, and she would never call her dad a liar, but inside she believed she was ugly and that he was only saying those things to make her feel better.

Erica's bubbly and outgoing nature began to change. Now that she believed she was ugly, she became shier, quieter, more self-conscious, and believed no one wanted to talk to an ugly girl or hear what she had to say. The truth was, while she had changed somewhat outwardly and was going through an awkward stage, she hadn't become ugly. Her hair was different, her body was beginning to mature, and like many kids her age, her face would occasionally break out. She believed the mean things the kids were saying rather than see the truth that stared back at her when she looked in the mirror. Erica no longer believed she was beautiful even though her dad consistently told her she was; she was haunted by the painful words the kids said to her.

Those children were completely unaware of how much power their words held. To them, they were just saying words to get attention, but Erica believed their words. Those ugly words became her new truth, and because of them, she lived her life differently. She lost her confidence and hesitated to speak up in class

or engage in conversations with new people. In fact, she rarely made eye contact with people anymore and would look at the ground instead. Her grades began to slip as well, because her sadness made it difficult for her to concentrate.

By the age of fourteen, Erica had grown up and matured quite a bit, and she began to change the way she viewed things, including herself. Over time, she came to see that the people who teased and bothered others were usually the ones who didn't feel good about themselves, and that those who were kind and compassionate were truly the most beautiful ones. The love of her family and friends helped her recognize the beauty that lay within her. She became more confident and outgoing, just like she had once been. Now, when her dad told her that she was the most beautiful girl in the world, she looked into his eyes and saw that this was the truth as he knew it. He wasn't lying, it was what he saw—and she believed him.

Erica began to excel in school again, and her confidence continued to grow. When she participated in class, she realized that her teachers and classmates valued what she had to say. She no longer cared about the opinions of the few students who used to tease her, and eventually they stopped. Erica knew that her opinion of herself was the one that mattered most, and she really liked the person she was becoming.

When a new girl transferred to her school, Erica overheard one of the boys making cruel remarks to her. She felt compelled to step in and put a stop to his behavior. She confronted the boy and told him that only an insecure person tries to bring others down. She also threatened to get him in trouble if he continued. There was no way she would allow what happened to her to become another person's story.

Erica fully understood the power of words. Words had the ability to badly hurt someone, but they also had the ability to heal a hurt friend, to make someone laugh, to inspire people, and to tell someone you love them. She decided that she would use this knowledge to teach others. She never forgot how bad she felt when she was teased as a child, and decided to become a teacher to educate children about using their words wisely. And that's just what she did.

Now Erica is a teacher, and she does not tolerate any student teasing another. She tells her students her own story and reminds them to choose their words carefully. A poster hangs in her classroom that reads, "Words are powerful, so use them wisely. Do not use them to crush others but instead to lift them higher." These are words she lives by. Each day Erica tells her students that she loves them and that they are the most beautiful children in the world. And they believe her, for they have no reason not to. These words are her truth.

Helpful Vocabulary Words and Discussion Questions for "The Most Beautiful Girl in the World"

Vocabulary words: infectious, deteriorate, unruly, pride, cascade, swoop, dramatic, insist, bubbly, crushed, self-conscious, outwardly, consistently, haunted, outgoing, transfer, cruel, compel, threaten, tolerate

Discussion Questions

1. If you have ever been teased or bullied like Erica was, what was your experience like, and how did you get past it?

2. Why do you think Erica never let her parents know she was being bullied?

3. While we all want to use our words wisely, sometimes we don't. How do you think we should handle the times when we or others say something hurtful?

STORY 5
It's Your Choice

"It's your choice." I remember my grandmother telling me those words one memorable day, and they've stayed with me ever since then. They were some of the wisest words anybody had ever said to me, but at first I thought my grandmother was confused or losing her mind. "Grandma, what are you talking about?" I asked her. "This kid is making fun of me. How is that my choice?"

Am I confusing you? Well, let me backtrack and tell you my story. It all started one Wednesday morning at school. I thought it was going to be a normal day, but boy, was I wrong. A new girl came into my class, and during lunch I thought I would introduce myself to her so she wouldn't feel alone and left out. I figured she could use a new friend.

"Hi, I'm Debbie," I said. "I just wanted to welcome you to our school." But the new girl wasn't very friendly or happy to meet me. Her exact words were, "I don't care what your name is. Why would you think I'd want to be friends with a loser like you?" My first thought was *ouch!* Then I wondered, *What's her problem?* What made it even worse was that some other kids started laughing. I decided I would stay clear of her from then on. I had just been trying to be nice and offer my friendship, but I guess she wanted to make friends on her own.

The next day, I didn't even go near her, but she started bothering me in the cafeteria. "Hey loser, why did you bother to come to school today? Nobody wants to hang around a loser like you." As if that weren't bad enough, the two friends she had already made were laughing at me, too.

Day after day, the abuse increased. The longer she was there, the more confident she became, and the worse I felt. One day I got so upset I told her, "Leave me alone! Why are you bothering me?" I started to cry, but she just laughed and called me a loser again.

This went on for two weeks, and it was wearing me down. I guess it was showing on my face because one day when I got home, my grandmother said, "You have not been yourself for quite a few days now. Are you going to tell me what's going on, Debbie?"

I said, "Grandma, there's this new girl at school. She's been there about two weeks, and she's making me miserable. She keeps calling me a loser, and now these other kids are laughing at me." Then she said those famous words to me: "It's your choice."

"Grandma, what are you talking about? This kid is making fun of me. How is that my choice?"

She smiled and said, "My dear child, we will never be able to control what anybody thinks or says about us. Although we would like everyone to like us, unfortunately, that's not going to happen, no matter how nice we are. There will always be folks who will be mean or lie about us or call us nasty names. But you have a choice whether or not to accept or believe those words. It's your choice whether you allow them to ruin your day or your mood. It's your choice whether or not you want to give them power. It's your choice whether to let those words go or hold on to them and let them hurt you. It's your choice."

I sat there for a few moments trying to comprehend her words. I had never thought of it that way. "So, Grandma, what you are saying is, I get to choose what to do with those words. I'm not powerless but powerful because I get to decide if it will bother me or not."

"Precisely," she said. "Sweetheart, know this, too. People who try to hurt others are usually in their own pain, and sometimes they don't even know it. They are usually more afraid than the people they pick on. So why should you believe a weak, fearful person's words?"

After Grandma gave me this profound advice, I felt bad for having contemplated that she was losing her mind. She was so much smarter than I knew. This became more apparent to me when I went to school the next day.

That day, just like every other day of the past two weeks, the girl called me a loser and her two friends started to laugh. But now I had made the decision not to let it bother me. Instead, I looked at her calmly and said, "I'm not a loser, but if

saying that makes you feel better, knock yourself out." She was taken aback; she hadn't expected me to answer her with confidence and power in my voice.

The next day, she called me a loser again. This time her friends didn't laugh, and I just smiled and walked away, saying, "Have a nice day."

On the third day, she looked at me but didn't say anything, and I knew that it was because I wasn't giving her words any power. When she saw that her words could not hurt me anymore, she realized there was no use in continuing, and she stopped.

I'm an adult now, but the words my grandma told me that day have always stayed with me. And she was right, I can't control how anybody behaves toward me, and I can't stop mean people from saying mean things. But it's my choice whether I want to believe them and let them bother me or not. I choose not to, and I'm happier in my life because of it.

Helpful Vocabulary Words and Discussion Questions for "It's Your Choice"

Vocabulary words: memorable, confused, backtrack, exact, confident, miserable, unfortunately, comprehend, powerless, precisely, profound, contemplate, apparent, aback, increase, respond, although, abuse, ruin, weak

Discussion Questions

1. Why did Debbie originally think that Grandma was confused when she told her, "It's your choice"?

2. Why were Grandma's words "It's your choice" so powerful? What do they teach us?

3. If you have ever been bullied, how did you handle the situation?

STORY 6
The Big, Ugly, Heavy Suitcase

On sunny summer days, the streets are always filled with kids enjoying their time off from school, and this day was no different. Chris, Hercules, and Michael, just back from riding their bikes, stopped by Hercules's house to get something cool to drink. They noticed Mr. Cycle, a sweet yet sad-looking gentleman, coming out of his house. What distinguished him from the other neighbors was that he had a very odd habit. Every time he came out of his house, he was carrying a big, ugly, heavy suitcase. Everyone could tell it was heavy by the way he lugged it around, and the patches it wore gave away its age.

Mr. Cycle never ventured far from his home because of the weight of the burdensome suitcase. Some days he got as far as the middle of the block and then turned around to head back home. One day he got as far as the corner, but then he turned right around, feeling exhausted by the enormous weight of the suitcase. Despite looking so sad, he was a kind and friendly man and was well liked by all of his neighbors. They would often offer to help him carry the suitcase, but he would refuse, saying he had to carry it on his own.

Like most of the neighbors, the children often wondered what was in the suitcase and why he was always carrying it. None of the neighbors ever asked, as they were respectful of Mr. Cycle's privacy, but this particular summer, the boys' curiosity had been building day by day.

Hercules said, "Maybe it's filled with gold coins he wants to take to the bank but it's too heavy for him to get all the way there. It would explain why he doesn't want anyone's help. He might be afraid they'd steal them."

"I don't think so," said Chris. "If that were the case, why wouldn't he just take some of the coins to the bank each day?"

"Good point, I never thought of that," said Hercules.

Michael said, "We could stand here coming up with theories forever and never know the truth. Let's politely ask the man. The worst-case scenario is he'll tell us to mind our own business."

The boys agreed and rode their bikes over to him. Michael asked, "Mr. Cycle, we are curious about that heavy suitcase you always carry. What's in there that's so heavy?" Mr. Cycle's sad expression turned to a warm smile. He looked at the boys and replied, "Well, I guess you could say it's filled with memories." Puzzled, the boys looked at one another and then at Mr. Cycle. They had never heard of anyone carrying their memories around in a suitcase.

"Let me show you," said Mr. Cycle as he began to open his bag. The boys waited with anticipation as he pulled out a heavy brick. He said, "This is one of the first memories I have. When I was just five years old and in kindergarten, a kid in my class told me my face was so ugly that it scared people."

"Really?" said Michael. "That was an awful thing to say. Well, your face doesn't scare us, Mr. Cycle. If it did, we would never have spoken to you, so obviously that kid was wrong. But why would you choose to hold on to that memory, especially since it seems painful and looks so heavy?"

"I don't know," said Mr. Cycle. "It has always made me feel miserable. I guess I thought I had to hold on to it."

"Well," said Hercules, "it happened so long ago, and that memory doesn't do you any good now. I would get rid of that one. If you do, I'm sure your suitcase will be easier to carry." Mr. Cycle agreed and decided to let that sad memory go, and the suitcase became lighter.

"What else is in there?" asked Chris. Mr. Cycle pulled out another brick. He said, "This one represents a time when I was twelve. I was playing baseball and accidentally hit the ball into my neighbor's car windshield. I felt so bad about it."

"I would feel awful about that too, but it was an accident," said Chris. "Everyone has them. I'm sure your neighbor knew you never intended to break it. Did you apologize?"

"Yes, I did," said Mr. Cycle. "And then I mowed the neighbor's lawn for the rest of the year to make up for the money it cost to repair the windshield. But I felt so guilty and ashamed, and I still do when I remember it."

"Mr. Cycle, it was an accident, and you acted responsibly by repaying your neighbor," said Hercules. "Why are you still carrying around that guilt? I think you should forgive yourself and let it go."

"I guess you're right. My neighbor did forgive me; it's time I forgave myself. I don't know why I held on to the guilt for so long."

He let that sad memory go, and the suitcase became even lighter. Mr. Cycle pulled out yet another heavy brick from his suitcase. "This one I have been carrying around since I was twenty-one years old. I was at my first job interview, and the man interviewing me told me I wasn't getting the job because I wasn't very knowledgeable about some matters the job required. I felt like such a failure; I can still remember the humiliation I felt."

"But Mr. Cycle, you had a good job for many years after that," said Michael. "I heard you were a head programmer for a computer company until you retired a few years ago. You obviously had a lot of knowledge to have that position for such a long time. Why would you hold on to the memory of a job you didn't get instead of the one you did?"

"I never thought of it that way. I don't think I need to carry that one anymore, either," Mr. Cycle said. He let that sad memory go, and the suitcase became still lighter.

It was beginning to get dark outside, and the boys knew it was time to go home. They decided to meet the next day to play baseball. Mr. Cycle was ready to go home, too. He now felt less sad, and he could walk much easier because his suitcase was so much lighter. He asked the boys to help him move the discarded bricks to the curb outside of his house.

Chris said, "Mr. Cycle, would you share some more memories with us tomorrow? We'd like to hear more stories." "I'd like that," he said. "You boys helped me feel much better today, and now my suitcase is so much easier to carry."

After playing baseball the next afternoon, the boys saw Mr. Cycle come out of his house carrying his suitcase. "Good afternoon, Mr. Cycle," called Michael. "How are you? Do you want some help carrying your suitcase?"

Mr. Cycle smiled at the boys. "I feel better today than I've felt in a long time, but I'm still feeling a bit blue. I appreciate your offer, but these are my memories, and only I can carry them."

"Maybe we can help you get rid of a few more unnecessary sad memories today," said Chris. "If we can't help you carry it, perhaps we can make the load easier for you to bear." Mr. Cycle nodded his head and began to open his suitcase. His eyes were smiling, as he was amazed by the kindness and consideration the boys were showing him. Although he had not yet taken out a brick from his suitcase, he was already feeling better inside.

The brick Mr. Cycle pulled out this time held a memory of a time he took a painting class. He explained that he had always loved going to museums and admiring the beautiful paintings. He wished he could create a painting that would bring somebody else as much joy as he felt. After weeks of the painting class, the students were asked to paint a bowl of fruit for their final project. "My project was just awful—the worst of the class," said Mr. Cycle. "One person said that my fruit looked like aliens. My instructor said I had shown some improvement, but I knew she was only trying to be nice. As hard as I tried, I couldn't make the painting better; it was a disaster."

"Well, if it makes you feel any better, Mr. Cycle, I can't draw either," said Michael. "Hercules is a great artist. He creates the most amazing comics, but I stink at it."

"But you're a great athlete, Michael, and I'm not," said Hercules. "Whenever they choose teams during gym class, I'm always the last one picked," he explained to Mr. Cycle. "My parents always remind me of the proverb, 'Nobody is good at everything, but everybody is good at something. Be prouder of your effort than the outcome.' Mr. Cycle, if you enjoy painting, then paint for yourself. I'm a terrible baseball player, but I love playing and won't ever give it up."

"I guess I thought that if I failed at something, it made me a failure. Thank you, boys. I'm going to get rid of this brick, too," said Mr. Cycle.

The next brick he took out of his suitcase was the biggest one yet. When the boys asked him about it, he said, "This one is my biggest fear. I am very afraid of being alone for the rest of my life. I have spent so much of my time working and trying to carry around this heavy suitcase that I haven't had the time or energy to keep up with old friends or make new ones."

"Well, Mr. Cycle, we'd like to think we're your friends now," said Chris. "You know, friends help one another; you don't need to carry your suitcase all by yourself. Let us help you, and let's get rid of that loneliness." Mr. Cycle's eyes filled with tears. "Thank you for offering me your friendship, and for all the help you boys have given me. I know I don't need to carry this brick with me anymore."

THE BIG, UGLY, HEAVY SUITCASE   47

As they sat and looked at the bricks still left in the suitcase, Mr. Cycle realized he no longer needed to carry any of the sad and heavy memories anymore. Once he pulled out the remaining bricks, he saw that they made a towering wall, one that had kept him from fully enjoying his life. The pain of all those memories had kept him trapped for years, unable to do all the things he had dreamed about. The big, ugly, heavy suitcase was finally empty, and he tossed it away along with the painful memories that had lived inside there for so long. He felt freer and happier than he had in years.

Mr. Cycle and the boys spent lots of time together that summer, and even went to a baseball game together. One day Michael asked him, "Mr. Cycle, how come there weren't any wonderful memories in your suitcase? Didn't you have any of those?" Mr. Cycle replied, "My dear boy, those I do have, but they've never weighed me down, for I've always carried them in my heart."

Helpful Vocabulary Words and Discussion Questions for "The Big, Ugly, Heavy Suitcase"

Vocabulary words: knowledgeable, programmer, distinguished, patches, venture, burdensome, enormous, privacy, curiosity, theories, scenario, anticipation, obvious, despite, ashamed, expression, require, humiliation, unnecessary, consideration

Discussion Questions

1. Why do you think Mr. Cycle carried around his negative memories for so long?

2. If you ever had a hard time letting go of a "heavy" memory, what helped you let go of it?

3. What is a happy memory that you carry in your heart?

PART III

Dealing with Guilt

STORY 7
The Race

Jackie was good—really good. But no matter how much she practiced running, she always came in second. She was frustrated once more after her last race, when Mary beat her again. Mary was always the best runner in the school, and probably in the entire county. But this time—this year—Jackie just had to win at the county championships. She wanted to know what it would feel like to be the best runner and get everyone's attention and admiration.

The girls were both on the track team at school, so they always practiced alongside each other and their teammates. Their coach encouraged both of them and pushed them to practice hard because they were his two best runners. Together, they helped make their track team the best it had been in years. Thus far this year, the team was undefeated.

All the girls on the track team got along, including Jackie and Mary, who had known each other since kindergarten and attended the same church. Despite always losing to Mary, Jackie really liked her because Mary was a wonderful girl and was good to everyone she encountered. But now that the county championship race was approaching, she couldn't help but feel resentment growing inside because she knew Mary was her biggest competition.

52   DEALING WITH GUILT

Jackie was always a determined girl. When she wanted to learn how to ride a two-wheeled bike, she convinced her cousin to take off the training wheels long before she was ready, and she rode that bike all day until she could ride it with ease. She didn't even mind the scrapes and bruises she acquired in the process that day.

Jackie's dad was also a runner. Back when he was in school, he was on the track team, too, but now he ran strictly for fun. The two of them would run together on weekends and spend the time chatting and enjoying each other's company. Jackie opened up to her dad about how much she wanted to win the big race and how worried she was about losing to Mary.

Her dad said, "Sweetheart, as long as you do your best, that's all that matters. Not many people are fortunate enough to have the talent to run that race. You should always strive to be your best, but whether you come in first, second, or last, I'll be proud of you." Even though her dad's words were soothing to hear and reminded her of how much she was loved, Jackie replied, "Thanks Dad, but I still want to win."

Jackie practiced intensely. She became fixated on her goal; it consumed her thoughts most of each day. The same questions played over and over in her mind. What would it be like to win? How would it feel to stand in front of all those people, get the trophy, and have her picture featured in the local paper? What would she do with the prize money? And then a thought came to her. *If I win, I'll give the prize money to my church to help build its community center.*

The next afternoon, as track practice was coming to a close, Mary said, "I guess I'll see you at the race this weekend. Do you know what time it starts?"

"Well, last year and the year before it began at one o'clock, so I think it would be at the same time," answered Jackie.

"Thanks," said Mary. "My parents and I are going away to visit my grandparents this weekend, and I want to make sure that we get back in time. I guess I'll see you Sunday at the sign-up table before the race."

"See you Sunday," said Jackie. "Have fun at your grandparents' house."

When Jackie got home later that day, she found a flier about the race in her mailbox. According to the flier, the race committee had decided to change the start time of the race because the weather forecasters were predicting rain for later in the afternoon, and the committee members wanted to fit in all the activities of the day. The time of the race was moved up to eleven o'clock.

Jackie grabbed her cell phone and started to call Mary to tell her, but then she stopped herself. *If she doesn't come, I'll surely win this year,* she thought. *It's almost guaranteed!* But her inner voice was telling her, *Make the call! It's the right thing to do. She's away this weekend, and there's no other way she could find out about the time change.* But she didn't call, and she put the phone down. However, her stomach felt upset the rest of the day.

Jackie woke up on Sunday morning and went for a short jog to warm up for the race. She was in the best shape she had ever been in, except for her stomach, which was still bothering her. Her inner voice kept telling her, *There's still enough time. Call Mary and let her know the new start time for the race.* But she continued to ignore it. Instead she popped in her headphones, blasted the music, and sang loudly to drown out her inner voice.

About an hour and a half before the race, as Jackie and her parents were getting ready to leave, her mom asked, "Honey, won't you please try and eat something before the race? You will need the energy to run. You barely ate any breakfast!"

"I'm not hungry, Mom," said Jackie. "My stomach is feeling really weird. It's probably just nerves." But she knew it wasn't her nerves. In fact, she rarely got nervous before a race; this feeling was something else. Then she heard her inner voice again. *You can still do the right thing. Call Mary and tell her about the time change.* But she didn't.

When she got to where the race was being held and went to register, she looked around to see if Mary was there. When she didn't see her anywhere in the crowd, she was more confident about her chances of winning, though she was feeling quite tense.

Mary didn't show up for the race, and Jackie won easily. After the race, she stood at the finish line with the medal around her neck. Everyone was cheering for her, just like she had hoped, and the local paper took her picture, just as she had imagined. But she wasn't feeling the joy she had expected to feel.

Her parents proudly stood by her as she announced that she was donating her prize money to her church's community center. Everyone was making a big deal over her, but Jackie was overwhelmed with guilt. Her stomach was not feeling any better even though she had won, and she kept looking around to see if Mary was going to show up. What would she say to her if she did?

Jackie's parents wanted to celebrate by taking her to her favorite restaurant for lunch, but she told them she was just too tired, and that she'd just prefer to go home. "Honey, are you okay?" her father asked. "I know you must be tired from the race, but I thought you'd be feeling a bit more energized and happy after your win."

"I'm fine, Dad. I guess the anxiety before the race and the excitement of winning just tired me out. I think I'd just like to go home and go to my room to rest."

Jackie didn't rest much, though; she kept thinking about Mary, and her stomach continued to bother her. How would she face her friend at school the next day? She thought of a few excuses she could use: "I thought you would have found out," or "I found out at the last minute, and it was too late to call you." They sounded good, but they didn't make her feel any better.

The next day, everyone was congratulating Jackie, including the school principal, who announced Jackie's win over the school's loudspeaker. Jackie hadn't seen Mary yet. At first, she worried that Mary might believe that she intentionally told her the wrong time. Jackie also imagined that Mary would guess the truth: that she withheld the time change from her to try and secure a win. *What if she figures it out and tells everyone,* she thought.

But Jackie was ashamed of herself. She had thought winning was everything, but now she realized that if a win is not truly earned, the victory is empty. Her guilt was eating her up inside, and the feeling in her stomach was proof of that. She knew she had to find Mary, apologize to her, and give up her title.

Then Mary was standing right in front of her, looking upset. Before she could say a word, Jackie blurted out, "I'm so sorry I didn't tell you about the time change so you could make it to the race. I wanted to win so badly, but I feel sick with guilt now. Please forgive me. I feel like I didn't deserve to win. I'm going to give up my title because I didn't win it fairly."

Mary said, "I forgive you for not calling me, and I do thank you for telling me the truth. But you don't have to give up your title. I found out about the change in time, but my grandfather got sick, and we ended up taking him to the hospital. That's why I wasn't at the race."

"I'm so sorry about your grandfather, Mary," Jackie said. "I hope he will be all right. And again, I'm sorry for not calling you. I thought winning was everything. Now I realize that if it's not a true win, the victory doesn't bring you any satisfaction."

"My grandfather will be fine; they had to remove his appendix, but he's already much better. As for you, I already told you I forgive you, and judging by how bad you look, I doubt you would do it again. You don't have to give up your title; it's yours. You earned it."

Jackie breathed a big sigh of relief. Mary said, "I heard that you gave away the prize money to our church for its community center. That's honorable. Now let go of your guilt and enjoy your win, because next year, I just might beat you." The two girls laughed.

As soon as Jackie got home, she confessed the truth to her parents. "Now we understand why you were acting so strange yesterday," said her mom. "Although we would have wanted you to do the right thing from the beginning, we are proud of you for telling Mary the truth and asking for her forgiveness. When we knowingly don't listen to our inner guidance voice, it usually leads to trouble and a guilty conscience. It's always better to trust in that voice and do the right thing from the beginning."

"I know that for sure now, Mom," Jackie said. "As soon as I did the right thing, it felt like a weight was lifted off of me. My stomach stopped bothering me, and I could finally eat."

"Okay then, lesson learned," said her dad. "Speaking of eating, I still think we should go out and celebrate your victory. After all, you truly did earn it."

The following year, Mary and Jackie ran in the county's annual race. This time, they tied for first place. Neither of them minded sharing the title of winner, and together they decided to give the prize money to their church's community center again. The local newspaper was there to take pictures of the girls standing side by side with beaming smiles. The reporter asked Jackie, "Do you mind not being the sole winner this year?" "Not at all," she replied. "In fact, this year's win is better and sweeter than I could have ever imagined."

Jackie never forgot the lesson she learned. She still always listens to her inner voice of guidance and is all the happier for it.

Helpful Vocabulary Words and Discussion Questions for "The Race"

Vocabulary words: admiration, alongside, encourage, honorable, determined, intensely, forecast, guarantee, predict, register, overwhelmed, prefer, energized, anxiety, resentment, appendix, sigh, conscience, acquire, strictly

Discussion Questions

1. Why couldn't Jackie enjoy herself when she won the race that Mary missed?
2. What did the experience teach her about herself?
3. If you have ever experienced a guilty conscience, how did it make you feel? How did you handle the situation?

STORY 8
The Guilt Bugs

From the time she was a toddler, Jamie was always seeking adventures. She loved to use her imagination and pretend that she was the captain of a ship or the chef at a famous restaurant, but this day she was imagining that she was an Olympic gymnast. She tumbled all around the bedroom she shared with her older sister, swinging up her arms and taking a bow for the adoring fans she pretended were watching her. She pictured them throwing beautiful flowers at her feet, and she graciously picked them up while throwing kisses to the crowd. She was really enjoying this glorious moment—until she swung up her arm and knocked her sister's spelling bee trophy off the shelf, accidentally breaking it.

"Oh no!" she cried. "Emily is going to be so mad. She loves that trophy." She thought about how proud her sister had been when she received the trophy at school the year before. Emily was always cleaning it and moving it from place to place, trying to find the perfect spot to showcase it. Any time a relative would come over to visit, she'd take them into her room and show it to them.

Jamie considered how she would tell her sister about breaking the trophy. She knew Emily would be home from school soon, so she had to think quickly. She thought, *What if I don't tell her? I'll just hide the trophy somewhere. Maybe she won't notice it missing.* She hid the trophy under her bed and hoped for the best.

When Emily came home that day, she went into the bedroom to drop off her school bag and then to the kitchen to get a snack. Jamie breathed a heavy sigh of relief when Emily hadn't noticed the missing trophy, but then she started feeling

a strange feeling in her tummy. She was unsettled by it because she had never felt this feeling before. It was a sinking feeling, as if her tummy were being pulled down by a heavy weight, but she didn't mention it to anyone. And then Jamie saw Emily heading to their bedroom.

Jamie started to panic. Emily always did her homework at her desk in their room, and she was certain that Emily would notice the missing trophy now. The feeling in her tummy got much worse, and so did her feeling of anxiety, yet she still didn't confess the truth. She decided to pretend nothing was wrong, and went to watch TV in the living room. As she sat there, she found it hard to concentrate on the show.

Suddenly, her head started to throb. Her mom came into the room and asked, "Are you okay? You have the strangest expression on your face."

"Mom, I'm not feeling that great right now."

Her mom felt her forehead and said, "You don't have a fever, but maybe you should sit on the couch and rest a while." Before Jamie could even get to the couch, she heard Emily call from their bedroom. "Jamie, come here. Where's my spelling bee trophy? Did you move it?"

Jamie's eyes opened wide, her heart began to race, and her tummy and head started to throb even more. She was afraid to tell her sister the truth, so she lied. "I don't know what happened to your trophy! Why would I know? Why are you asking me? Maybe you put it someplace and don't remember. You are always moving it around. I had nothing to do with it."

Emily recognized the guilt in Jamie's voice and expression, but she couldn't prove that Jamie had anything to do with the trophy's disappearance. She decided to wait a while to see if Jamie would tell the truth. "Okay, Jamie, I'll ask Mom and Dad if they have seen it. If they don't know, then we will all start searching for it together."

Jamie wanted to feel better. It seemed as if Emily believed her, but that made her feel even worse. Her stomach was in knots, her head was pounding, and the guilt she felt inside was torturing her. She knew she would continue to feel worse if she didn't tell the truth.

Jamie went into the living room, where Emily was talking with their mom. When her mom asked her if she was feeling better, Jamie answered, "No, I feel awful." Her mother had a suspicion that her ill feelings had something to do with the missing trophy, but she suggested that Jamie lie down and take a nap.

After uncomfortably tossing and turning for a while, Jamie finally fell asleep. She began to hear a strange buzzing sound. She looked around and saw what looked like a huge mosquito. Then she heard a voice say, "You broke the trophy." She thought it was Emily accusing her and screamed, "No, I didn't," but she realized that no one was in the room with her except the annoying bug that continued to circle around her. Suddenly, a second big bug was buzzing around her, and she heard a voice say, "You're lying." Jamie couldn't believe it; the bugs were talking to her, and they knew what had happened.

She thought she was losing her mind. *How could the bugs be talking to me? How do they know I broke the trophy and lied to my sister about it? Did they see what happened?* She began to panic as the bugs circled around her faster and faster, buzzing and accusing her of lying and breaking the trophy. She couldn't handle

62 DEALING WITH GUILT

it anymore and began to cry and scream, "I did it, I did it. I broke the trophy, and I lied!" Then the bugs disappeared, and she woke up.

Her mom and sister heard her screaming and ran into the room. They comforted her and assured her that she was just having a bad dream. Once Jamie stopped shaking, she explained that she was dreaming that two giant bugs were attacking her and yelling at her. Emily brought her a glass of water and asked, "Do you feel better now? You know bugs can't talk. It was just a bad dream."

"Emily, it seemed so real," Jamie said.

Her mother asked, "What on earth were the bugs yelling at you?"

Jamie looked at her sister and said, "Emily, I accidentally broke your trophy. I'm sorry I lied to you. I was just scared that you'd get mad at me and that I'd get in trouble. The bugs in my dream knew what I had done and were calling me a liar."

"Sweetheart," their mom said, "I think there is a reason you had that nightmare. Sometimes, when we feel guilty because we have done something wrong, it starts to affect our health. Our conscience, which is the voice of truth inside of us, gets very uncomfortable. The guilt we feel can upset our stomach, our head, and can even affect our sleep. In your case, it caused you to have a bad dream."

"So, what did you do to the bugs in your dream? Did you try to swat them?" asked Emily.

"No, I just confessed, and they disappeared." Her mom smiled at her and said, "I guess they were a couple of 'Guilt Bugs.' Once the guilt disappeared, they did, too. That's where the saying 'The truth shall set you free' comes from."

Emily chuckled. "I guess telling the truth worked like bug spray in your dream." They all laughed. Jamie apologized once more to Emily for breaking the trophy and for lying to her, and her sister graciously forgave her.

Although Jamie ended up losing her TV privileges that night for lying to her sister, it didn't bother her very much. She preferred that punishment over the anguish her guilty feelings had been causing her. The two girls glued the trophy back together, and fortunately, it looked as good as new. Soon it was back on the shelf, where it stood as a daily reminder to Jamie to always be honest and keep the Guilt Bugs away.

Helpful Vocabulary Words and Discussion Questions for "The Guilt Bugs"

Vocabulary words: toddler, tumble, adoring, gracious, glorious, showcase, relieved, unsettled, concentrate, recognize, pounding, accuse, panic, comfort, nightmare, affect, anguish, privileges, reminder, throb

Discussion Questions

1, How did Jamie's guilt about lying to Emily affect her?

2. Why didn't Jamie mind losing her television privileges as a punishment?

3. Before Jamie confessed, Emily didn't continue to question Jamie about the trophy even though she knew Jamie was lying. She was even kind to Jamie and brought her a glass of water after she had a bad dream. What does this tell us about Emily's character and their relationship as sisters?

PART IV

Facing Fear

STORY 9
The What-If Monster

Eva heard the moving truck drive up to the front of her house—another reminder of how many things were changing in her life right now. She didn't want to move away from her home, her school, and especially her friends, but sometimes life doesn't leave any options. The company her dad worked for was relocating to a different state, so the family needed to move with the company.

Her dad had left the month before to find the family a place to live while Eva finished up the school year. Her mom had gone to visit him for a few days and to interview for a teaching job for the fall. She seemed happy about the move, and her dad was fine with it, too. Eva's baby sister, Julie, only three and a half years old, didn't understand the changes that were occurring, but to nine-year-old Eva, life was now confusing and scary.

Eva, Julie, and their mom made the two-hour drive to their new home, where her dad was excitedly waiting for them. The house, which smelled of fresh paint, was nice, but it was much smaller than their old home, and so was the yard.

There were boxes everywhere. As Eva walked around to examine her new surroundings, she heard a familiar voice. She recognized it as the voice of her great-aunt Millie. She had only met Aunt Millie a few times, when she had come to visit on holidays, so Eva didn't know her very well, but Aunt Millie's warm smile and beautiful costume jewelry had left an impression on Eva. She always wore such lovely jewelry to match her outfits.

"Eva, come here, my sweet, and give your Aunt Millie a hug. You've grown so much since I last saw you." Eva welcomed her with a big hug and a kiss. It was comforting to see a familiar face among her new surroundings.

Aunt Millie squeezed her tightly and said, "We're going to be spending a lot more time together now that you have moved closer to me. I'm so thrilled to have my family nearby; it makes my heart smile."

That night, after a delicious pizza dinner, Eva went up to her new room to sleep. Her parents had set up her bed and had even gone to the trouble of having her new room painted the very same shade of purple as her old room to make her feel more comfortable. Even though she was in her same bed, with the same sheets and pillow she had before, she had trouble falling asleep, because although her room was quiet, her mind was not. She was distressed by the many questions that kept popping into her head. Every question started with the same two words, "What if?"

What if people here aren't friendly? What if the kids in the neighborhood are mean and I don't make any friends? What if I don't like my new school or my new teacher? What if I hate it here?

All these questions and more escalated her anxiety and prevented her from getting much sleep. Her restless night was evident in her face the next morning, because as soon as she walked into the kitchen, Aunt Millie said, "Good morning, sweetie. Did you not sleep well last night? You look tired."

"Not really," replied Eva. "Where are my mom and dad?"

"They went to the market to pick up a few things. Come sit next to me and tell me what kept you from enjoying a good night's sleep."

Eva sat down and started telling Aunt Millie about all the questions that had been popping into her head the night before, and then she began to cry.

"Oh, my sweet girl, I know how scary change can be. When I was a young girl, my father was in the military, and I had to move three times. I had to leave my home, my friends, and my school and start over in a new place every time, so I'm familiar with that old 'what-if' monster that invades your mind. That's what I called it because all those what-if questions would just scare me to death."

"Aunt Millie, what did you do to get that monster out of your head?" asked Eva.

Aunt Millie shook her head and said, "Well, my love, the truth is that the monster never completely leaves your head. It likes to pop in to scare you any time you're facing something new or different in your life."

"Oh no! I'm never going to sleep again," said Eva.

"You will, my dear, and I'm going to tell you how," said Aunt Millie. "You see, that what-if monster isn't real and doesn't have any real power. It only scares us if we let it. What I've learned is that when scary thoughts come into your mind, you don't have to let them live there. The first thing I do is try to replace the scary what-if questions with happy ones, like, 'What if this is the best day of my life? What if today is filled with wonderful surprises?' That automatically makes me feel a little better. Then I put a smile on my face, even if I'm still nervous. It helps me to relax a little. Then I take a deep breath and remind myself that we are never given any more than we can handle, that I will get past this, and that everything will be okay. And it usually is. Most of the time, the what-if monster tries to scare us about things that never happen. So why should I spend time being afraid of something that might never happen?"

"But what if what you're afraid of does happen, Aunt Millie? Then what do you do?"

"Well," Aunt Millie said, "I've been alive a lot longer than you, and sometimes things don't always turn out just the way we want them. Sometimes things happen to teach us something new about ourselves, like how strong we really are. But lots of times, what we get turns out to be better than what we wanted in the first place. Eva, you are blessed with a family who loves you very much, and when you have love around you, you have access to extra strength you never knew you had, and you can handle much more than you can imagine."

Eva felt better after talking to Aunt Millie, and that night she slept much better. The conversation didn't take away all her fears, and some nights the what-if monster reappeared, but she remembered Aunt Millie's advice, and it helped. She spent a lot of time with Aunt Millie that summer and grew to adore her. She realized that even the scariest changes in life can bring wonderful blessings, because moving to this new home brought her sweet Aunt Millie into her life, and that change was one of the best things that ever happened to her.

Helpful Vocabulary Words and Discussion Questions for "The What-If Monster"

Vocabulary words: evident, neighborhood, distressed, options, relocate, interview, occur, thrilled, escalate, prevent, restless, automatic, conversation, costume jewelry, surroundings, nearby, invade, military, shade, reappear

Discussion Questions

1. If you have ever felt nervous or anxious before a big change in your life, how did the actual experience compare to what you expected or feared?

2. Eva's new adventure led to her having a wonderful relationship with Aunt Millie. What positive effects resulted from your big change?

3. What helpful advice would you give somebody when the what-if monster starts to bother them?

STORY 10
Do It Afraid

There were two things eight-year-old Jennifer loved to do: watch baseball with her dad and dance. Her mom told her that she started dancing even before she began to walk. In fact, the only time Jennifer wasn't dancing was when she was in school. When she woke up every morning, she turned on her radio and danced as she made her bed, and then kept on dancing as she dressed for school. She even wiggled around in her chair as she ate breakfast.

This morning she danced around even happier than usual, as today she was going to take her first official dance class. After gobbling down her oatmeal, she announced to her mom that she was ready to leave.

Jennifer really enjoyed her first lesson. The teacher was friendly, and the other girls in her class were so nice. She couldn't wait until the following Saturday to do it again. By the third week, she felt like she had always been a part of the class and was excited to have made new friends.

The girls in her dance class began spending time together socially, as their parents planned playdates for them. At one of these playdates, Jennifer started to notice some differences between herself and the other girls. Two of the girls, Megan and Stephanie, were having a discussion about their favorite musical group. The rest of the girls chimed in on the discussion and talked about how much they loved their music and how they wished they could see their favorite group in concert. Although Jennifer didn't particularly care for the group, she just agreed with the others and said, "Oh yes, I love their songs, too." She was afraid to admit that she didn't like that group, as she didn't want to upset her friends or feel left out.

Later that day, while the girls were having lunch, Megan's mom set out apple juice and orange juice for them. Jennifer noticed that all the other girls preferred the apple juice, so she poured herself a glass despite the fact that she didn't like apple juice. Her mom noticed but didn't ask her about it.

The playdate was just about over when Stephanie's mom announced to the girls that she had just found out that their beloved musical group would be performing in their town the next month. She told the girls that if they were interested in going, she would find out if there were tickets available, and they could all go. All the girls were very excited about going to the concert—except Jennifer. Not only did she not like the group, but on that particular day, she and her dad had planned to attend a baseball game together. Instead of saying she didn't want to go, she said, "Sure."

On their way home, Jennifer's mom said, "Jenn, I know you don't like that group's music. And did you forget that you and Dad had planned to attend a baseball game the same day as the concert?"

"No, I didn't forget, Mom. I just thought that Dad wouldn't mind if I went to the concert with my friends instead," she answered.

"Sweetheart, it wouldn't be very nice of you to cancel your plans with your dad. He's been looking forward to going with you to that game for a long time, and he thought you were looking forward to it, too. He cleared his work schedule and went to a lot of trouble to get those tickets so he could share that special time with you. It's not nice to cancel on someone when you've made a commitment to them. That would really hurt his feelings."

Jennifer's head dropped. "I don't want to hurt his feelings. I want to go the game, but . . ."

Her mom looked over to her and said, "Honey, I know you want to be liked by your friends and you want to fit in with the group, but I also know you don't even like that group—and you hate apple juice, too."

Jennifer's eyes filled with tears. "Mom, you're right, I don't like that group's songs and I can't stand apple juice, but I really like my friends, and I want them to like me." She began to cry.

"Everyone wants to be liked, especially by their friends. But it's more important to stay true to yourself and be liked and accepted for who you really are. You have to be honest with your friends. If they won't accept you for who you are, then they are not truly your friends."

Jennifer knew that canceling on her dad would be an awful thing to do, and she never wanted to disappoint him. She really wanted to go the baseball game, but she was also nervous about being honest with her friends. But she knew she had to do the right thing and honor her commitment to her dad and tell the girls the truth. She wondered how they would react, and kept imagining various outcomes. The more she thought about it, the more scared she felt. She didn't sleep very well that night, especially knowing that she would see the girls at dance class the next day.

As her mom drove her to her class, Jennifer remembered a conversation she had once had with her dad while they were watching a baseball game. It was an important playoff game, and it was almost over. There was a lot of pressure on the players to win, and she wondered if they were feeling as nervous as she was just watching. She had asked her dad, "Aren't the players afraid of losing and disappointing their fans? How do they do it?" Her father had replied, "They do it afraid. They feel the fear and simply do their best, whether it makes their fans happy or not." She now decided to do the right thing, afraid.

Jennifer entered the studio and waved as she walked over to the girls. After they exchanged hellos, she took a deep breath and admitted to them all the things she had been misleading them about. She told them she didn't want to go to the concert because she wasn't a fan of the group. She said that she loved baseball and was going to a game with her dad instead. She also told them that she couldn't stand apple juice.

The girls were puzzled and asked her why she hadn't mentioned these things before. When Jennifer told them she was afraid of feeling left out, they assured her that it didn't change how they felt about her. All the anxiety and fear she had been feeling melted away. Megan even told her that she was a big baseball fan, too, and that she played on a softball team. She asked Jennifer if she'd like to come see her team play some time.

Jennifer and her dad ended up having a wonderful time at the baseball game. In fact, it was one of the most exciting games they had ever watched, which only made her love the game more. And not only did Jennifer go watch Megan play softball, but she eventually ended up joining the team, and the rest of the girls from the dance class became part of their regular cheering section.

Helpful Vocabulary Words and Discussion Questions for "Do It Afraid"

Vocabulary words: eventually, mention, puzzled, awful, gobbling, announce, official, socially, chimed in, particularly, admit, except, schedule, outcome, various, pressure, exchange, misleading, concert, beloved

Discussion Questions

1. Why was Jennifer initially more interested in being accepted by her friends than concerned about disappointing her father?

2. If you have ever been afraid to be completely honest about your likes or dislikes with your friends, how did you handle it?

3. What would you say to your friends to help them feel more comfortable being completely honest about their likes and dislikes?

STORY 11
The Truth Behind Their Words

Alex and John had been friends since they met in kindergarten. The summer before sixth grade, Alex went away to visit his grandparents in New York, while John went to a local camp for a few weeks. When the summer was over, the boys couldn't wait to catch up on their summer tales.

Alex spoke about all the exciting sites he and his grandparents visited in New York. John, on the other hand, shared adventures he had had with new friends he made at camp. He had met a group of boys who were a year older and went to the same school where he and Alex would be attending in the fall. He had played lots of basketball with them, and they had encouraged him to try out for the school's basketball team.

The first week of the school year always brings excitement and anxiety, but when it means attending a new school, these feelings can be heightened. Alex and John didn't know their way around the school building, and they didn't know any of the teachers or staff or many of the students. Fortunately, they were in a few of the same classes, which helped make the adjustment more comfortable.

When John encountered some of his camp friends in the hallway, they reminded him to not miss basketball tryouts the following week. He went to the tryouts and made the basketball team, and both he and Alex were happy. Alex told John that he would come to every game to cheer him on.

At his first game, John scored twelve points, and his teammates were thrilled, as was his coach. Just as promised, Alex was in the stands cheering him on. When the game was over, he went over and congratulated John and told him he would treat him to some celebratory ice cream. While John appreciated the offer, he told his friend that the team had a tradition of going out for pizza after their games. He invited Alex to join them, but Alex didn't feel comfortable going because he wasn't part of the team. He said, "That's okay, go have fun. I'll see you tomorrow."

Although Alex really did want John to celebrate how well he played and was genuinely happy that John was making new friends, he couldn't help but feel left out. He just shrugged it off and thought, "Well it's no big deal. He's still my best friend, and it will always be that way."

The boys met up the next morning and walked to school together, just as they always had. But over the next couple of months, they spent less and less time together. It seemed that between studying, practice, and basketball games, John had almost no free time to spend with Alex. Although John did miss spending time with his best friend, his schedule was so full that he barely had time to notice just how much he missed Alex.

Alex, on the other hand, was experiencing something completely different. It really started to bother him that John had become so bonded with the other players on the basketball team. Although Alex didn't really know those kids, he resented them and felt as if they were taking his friend away from him.

John and Alex still walked to school together, but they didn't talk as much as they used to. They spoke about their schoolwork, but they never talked about basketball anymore. Then Alex started skipping John's games. The first time he missed one, he told John he had lots of studying to do, but it wasn't the truth. The truth was that Alex was jealous of the relationships John had built with the other boys on the team. He got the idea in his head that John's friendships with the players took something away from theirs, making it less important or special. After missing four games in a row, he stopped making excuses. John had no clue what Alex was feeling and wondered if his old friend just didn't care about him anymore.

Both boys were upset and wondered how their long-time friendship had unraveled, but neither one told the other how he felt or how much he missed spending time together. Instead, they both silently let their pain grow inside of them, and the results were not pleasant.

One morning, as the boys were walking to school, the pain and fear they were each feeling broke out in the form of an argument. It started when John told Alex that the basketball team might make it to the playoffs. John hoped Alex would be happy for him, but all Alex could think about was that John's team had taken his friend away from him. He said, "I'm sure your friends are happy for you."

John asked him, "Aren't you happy for me? Aren't you my friend?" Alex wanted to be happy for him. He wanted to say, "Yes, of course. You're my best friend," but the fear, hurt, and insecurity that had been haunting him stopped him. He thought, *What if he doesn't consider me his best friend anymore? What if his teammates are now?* Instead of telling John the truth, Alex said, "I don't want to hear about your team anymore. I just don't care."

John was devastated and thought Alex no longer cared about him. He said, "Well I don't care if you ever come to another game again." They didn't speak the rest of the way to school nor for the next two days.

Both boys were hurting, and neither one knew that the other was even in pain; they could only feel their own. At home, both sets of parents noticed that the boys were not themselves, but when they asked their sons if anything was bothering them, both John and Alex told their parents they were just tired from studying for midterms. Their parents had no reason to doubt them and told them to get some extra rest over the long weekend coming up.

That Sunday, Alex's Uncle Vincent was hosting a party for his friends and family at his new house. Alex was excited because not only would he get to see his uncle's new place, he also loved spending time with him.

As soon as Alex came in, his uncle gave him a big bear hug and took him on a tour. While they walked through the house, Uncle Vincent mentioned that John and his family were coming over, too. Though Alex did not utter a word, his uncle saw his reaction and knew something had happened between the two boys. After some prodding, Uncle Vincent got Alex to tell him what was going on with their friendship, and then he could see what the true issue was between the boys.

Uncle Vincent sat his nephew down and said, "You know, this is not really about the basketball team; it's about your fear of losing your best friend. And I'll bet John is feeling the same way right now. Sometimes we need to consider the emotions behind what people say instead of just focusing on the words coming out of their mouths, because they can be two different things. I'm sure you're really proud of how well John is playing and how he's helping his team, aren't you?"

"Yes, I am really proud of him," replied Alex.

"But instead of telling him that, you said, 'I don't care.' What you really want is to spend time with your best friend. You're just letting your fear of losing him do the talking. I'll bet John is hurt that you're not going to his games and is afraid you don't care about him anymore."

"I never thought of it that way, Uncle Vincent. He spends so much time with his team, and I feel left out."

"You know, you aren't in a competition with others for his friendship. Just because some new friends came into John's life doesn't mean he cares less about you. The heart has an infinite capacity to love and more than enough room to accommodate lots of friends. Not having the opportunity to spend as much time with someone as you used to doesn't mean that the spot they hold in your heart is any smaller. You don't love your grandparents any less when they go away in the summer, do you?"

"Of course not," said Alex.

"What is important," Uncle Vincent continued, "is to treasure the time you do have with the people you care about. I think you should tell John the truth: you just miss spending time with him."

Uncle Vincent always knew how to help Alex uncover and resolve whatever issues he was facing, which was one of the reasons Alex always felt so close to him. After processing his uncle's words for a while, Alex knew he had to muster the courage to speak to John and let him know how he was feeling.

Later that day, when John showed up to the party, Alex went right over to speak to him. "John, I want to apologize for acting so childish. I really am proud of you for making the playoffs. I was just acting that way because I was scared that I was losing my best friend. I felt left out."

"Really?" said John. "I never wanted you to feel left out. When you stopped coming to my games, I thought you didn't care about me and didn't want to be my best friend anymore."

The boys reconciled and spent the afternoon catching up, just like old times. They made a pact that if something ever started to bother either one of them again, they would deal with the issue immediately instead of ignoring it. Now they are college roommates, and they have kept their pact to this day.

Helpful Vocabulary Words and Discussion Questions for "The Truth Behind Their Words"

Vocabulary words: adjustment, celebratory, shrug, barely, bonded, resent, jealous, unravel, insecure, devastated, reaction, prod, accommodate, opportunity, resolve, muster, reconcile, process, heighten, genuine

Discussion Questions

1. Why was it difficult for Alex and John to talk to each other about their conflict?

2. If you have ever had a misunderstanding with a friend, how did you resolve it?

3. Friends can grow apart for many different reasons. If this has ever happened to you, how did you handle it?

PART V

Being Your Best and Not Comparing Yourself to Others

STORY 12
Let Your Light Shine

Peter was born special and was the beautiful child his parents had always wanted. He had a twinkling light in his eyes that let the world know he was extraordinary. Very early on, people saw that he had a special gift: he learned quickly and was quite articulate at a very young age. By the age of two he was reading with ease. At five years old, he could work the cash register at his father's store, even at the busiest of times.

When Peter started kindergarten, he immediately stood out from his classmates. His teacher and the school's principal knew he was beyond the academic level of his peers. This was before schools had advanced specialty classes, so they had Peter skip a grade and moved him into a class of children who were a year older.

Although Peter had advanced a grade, he was still not challenged enough. He skipped another grade, and he finally felt truly challenged. For the rest of the year he was in a class with children two years older than him. The following year, he again skipped a grade.

Peter excelled in school and was an honor roll student, but now some of his classmates were beginning to tease him about his intelligence—and his height. Of course, being three years younger than everyone else made him the shortest kid in the class. He couldn't do anything about his height, but he could do something about his grades.

Peter didn't want to be different. He didn't like being teased and called a smarty-pants or a show-off, so he started to downplay his intelligence. He stopped trying to excel in his classes. He did his homework but didn't study much. He thought, *I just want to be like everyone else*. The twinkle in his eyes that had once sparkled so brightly was dimming.

Peter's younger sister, Maria, was bright but not as gifted as he was. He always helped her with her homework, especially her assignments on current events. Maria felt lucky to have such a smart brother but wondered why she never saw him study. He would tell his parents he was studying in his room, but whenever Maria would go in for homework help, she saw him doing other things. One day she said, "Peter, you are so smart, but you never study anymore. Your grades are good, but they're not the best. Why aren't you trying more? Are you just being lazy?"

Peter looked at her and said, "No, Maria, you just don't understand. I'm tired of the kids in my class making fun of me. Some of them teased me when I was getting the best grades in the class. I don't want to be teased. I don't want to stand out. I just want to be accepted. I want to be just like everybody else!"

Maria was puzzled. She said, "So many people wish they had your ability. They have to work two or three times as hard to do what you can do without even trying. You are not supposed to be like everyone else. Everybody has something about them—their own combination of gifts and talents—that makes them special. You are smarter than me, but I sing better. I'm not going to start singing badly to make you feel better when you sing; that would be ridiculous. Mom and Dad always say that you have to let the light inside of you shine so that you can become all you are meant to be."

Deep down in his heart, Peter knew his sister was right, but still he thought, *Why should I work harder and then end up getting teased for it? Is it really worth the trouble? I enjoy not being harassed more than I ever enjoyed having the best grades.*

Peter continued to put a minimal amount of effort into his schoolwork. He was now getting average grades, but this didn't bother him in the least. His teachers and parents constantly encouraged him to push himself more, but they couldn't make him do it.

When Peter began middle school, his shorter height was even more noticeable, as the other kids towered over him. But he grew taller over the year, and his height became less of an issue. Because he was still so much younger than the other kids, many of them weren't eager to be his friend, but eventually Peter's kind and warm personality and his great sense of humor helped him attract some wonderful friends.

In the beginning of his second year in middle school, Peter began to notice a change in many of the other students. He saw that they were working harder and trying to get good grades. He had been hiding his ability to get excellent grades for years so as to not be ostracized, but now it seemed that being really smart was no longer a negative trait. He wondered, *Would people treat me differently if I did try my best? Or would they start ridiculing me again? And should I even care?* He realized that he no longer wanted to live his life for anyone else's approval. That year was a turning point in Peter's life, and the changes were reinforced after he had the opportunity to meet his idol.

Peter's school hosted a Career Day for the students each spring, and this year, former alumnus and pro baseball player Zach Madden was going to visit. Madden, Peter's favorite baseball player, played for the New York Nationals baseball team. In fact, Peter had Zach's posters all over his room and watched every game he could on TV. He and his dad were Zach's biggest fans. He found it thrilling that Zach Madden was actually going to visit his school.

When Career Day finally arrived, Peter thought he would burst from excitement. And then, there he was—Zach Madden. From the stage, Madden spoke about how much he loved school not only because he was on the baseball team but also because he had loved his science classes. He said that he had always loved to play baseball, and while he was one of the best players on the team, he was not *the* best. He became better because he pushed himself all the time. "I always wanted to be proud of the effort I put into my work. Even if I wasn't the best at something, I wanted to be *my* best at it."

Madden talked about his love for science and admitted that someday, after he retired from baseball, he wanted to pursue a career in science. He spoke about belonging to the science club in school and shared stories about different inventions he and the other members worked on. He said, "Sometimes we were teased for our inventions, but we didn't let it get to us. Always be proud and celebrate who you are. Your passions and your gifts are what make you different and special. Never give them up just because somebody else doesn't think they're cool. Just do your best and let yourself shine." As Peter sat and listened to his hero, he realized that much of what Madden was saying was what his parents and sister had said to him.

Madden's words resonated with Peter long after he finished speaking. He decided to start doing his best at everything, and he did just that. His grades shot back up to straight A's, and he made the dean's list every term. His teachers, parents, and sister were proud of him, but more importantly, he was proud of himself. He never again let anyone's words dim the light that radiated from inside himself.

Today Peter is in his fifties and successfully manages his family's real estate property. His eyes still sparkle, and his inner light shines as brightly as ever.

Helpful Vocabulary Words and Discussion Questions for "Let Your Light Shine"

Vocabulary words: extraordinary, articulate, peers, intelligence, excel, sparkle, gifted, harass, minimal, average, ostracize, ridicule, invention, pursue, accept, constantly, approval, alumnus, resonate, immediately

Discussion Questions

1. Why didn't Peter listen to Maria's advice even when he knew deep down in his heart she was right?

2. Why did Peter change his mind once he heard his hero, Zach Madden, speak?

3. Talk about someone in your life who encourages you to be your best. What advice have they given you?

STORY 13
Not Like Everybody Else

When I was a little girl, I wanted to be just like everybody else, until my mother showed me why I shouldn't. On the third Friday of every month, our school had Dress Down Day, which meant we didn't have to wear our school uniform and could wear whatever we wanted. I loved those days because I always thought our school uniform was so ugly.

Since Dress Down Day happened only once a month, it was a special treat. I would look through my entire closet and choose my newest and coolest outfit that I hadn't yet worn to school. I would wake up so excited that I couldn't wait to go to school and let everyone see how great I looked in my own clothes instead of the school uniform.

That all changed one Friday in May when I was in fifth grade. The day started out like every other Dress Down Day. I had chosen my outfit the night before and put it on the chair next to my bed. It was a birthday gift I had received just the week before from my godmother, who always looked amazing herself. I squealed with delight when I opened box and saw the white denim outfit: white jeans, a matching jean jacket, and a T-shirt with a glittery silver heart on it. I really loved the outfit and couldn't wait to wear it. My godmother included a note that read, "I really hope you like your gift, Patti!"

That morning I walked into the classroom with a big smile, beaming and feeling great. Then I looked around and noticed that all the other girls—*everyone!*—

was wearing dark blue designer jeans! I had seen these jeans in department stores and on TV commercials, and although they looked really cool, they were also really expensive. Everyone was giggling and talking about how much they liked each other's jeans, even though they looked like they were all wearing the same exact ones. My white denim outfit stood out in the worst way, and I hated the feeling that gave me. I felt left out and didn't like my outfit anymore.

My friend Helen came over and told me she thought I looked nice, but I was sure she was just trying to make me feel better. Nobody else complimented me — *nobody!* I went home at the end of the day feeling devastated.

Moms have what I call a "special radar," which means they immediately know when something is bothering their child. Although I didn't speak a word about it when I got home that day, my mom could sense that something was troubling me.

After a little prodding from her, I told her what had happened at school, and then asked if she would take me shopping to buy a pair of dark denim designer jeans. Although my mom would do almost anything to make me happy, she said no.

"Patti, I could not afford to buy you those jeans even if I wanted to," she said. "But even if I could, I would be buying them for the wrong reason. You never once asked for them or even showed the slightest interest in getting them before. You only want them now because everybody else has them. That's not a reason to buy something, especially when it's out of our budget. Besides, you should always strive to be a unique individual. How boring would it be if everyone looked exactly like everyone else? How would we be able to tell anyone apart? Be who you are meant to be, and dress in clothes you like; that's how you express your individuality. Like a fine piece of art, the value of something is in the original, not a copy. In time, you will understand that people recognize and appreciate you for that more than for copying others."

"But Mom, today I was wearing my new white jeans outfit, and nobody appreciated how unique and different I looked. All the girls were just talking to each other about how much they liked each other's jeans. They didn't even pay attention to my clothes. Only Helen said I looked nice, and I think she did that just to make me feel better."

"Well," Mom said, "you don't know that Helen said that to make you feel better, you're making that assumption because of how you felt once you realized that you were dressed differently from everyone else. And I'll bet that changed your whole demeanor today. Patti, you loved that outfit when your godmother gave it to you, and you were so excited to wear it today. You were beaming this morning as you left, full of confidence and joy. That feeling, that confidence, is what people notice."

"A person who loves who they are inside and feels good in whatever they wear will make an impression on others. The secret is in the way you carry yourself. A person could wear an outfit made of paper bags, but if they like it and feel confident, people will be attracted to them because of that attitude. Be proud of your choices in outfits; you should never feel embarrassed or insecure because they're different."

"I guess so." I knew what she said made sense, but I still felt sad. I thought, *Well, tomorrow we go back to wearing our uniform, and for once I'll be happy to wear that ugly old thing.*

The next day, nobody talked about Dress Down Day, and I was thrilled. Now I knew it was silly of me to have gotten so upset about not having the same jeans as everybody else; I guess I just didn't want to feel left out. But everybody was busy with their everyday school routines, and nobody treated me any differently. Honestly, I don't think they even cared. I wondered why it seemed like such a big deal to me the day before. Maybe Mom was right.

Weeks passed, and the next Dress Down Day was approaching. I knew I wasn't going to be wearing the dark denim designer jeans that everybody else would likely wear again, but I accepted that. I wasn't treated any differently after I wore my white denim jeans the previous month, so I decided to wear something that was going to make me happy and not worry about what everyone else would be wearing.

When I got home, I was surprised to see my mom doing something on her sewing machine. She only occasionally used it, usually just to hem pants, but I saw that she was holding my red jeans. They had already been hemmed, so I asked, "Mom, what are you doing with my red jeans?"

"I wanted to surprise you," she answered. "Take a look at them." She had sewn a beautiful letter P on one of the pockets and added lovely designs on the others. They looked incredible!

"I knew you wanted to wear these to school tomorrow, and I knew how sad you felt last month when you were the only one who did not have a pair of designer jeans," Mom said. "Now you have a one-of-a-kind pair of designer jeans with your initial on them. They are as different and special as you are."

I hugged my mother tightly and said, "They are so beautiful! Thank you, Mommy, for loving me so much and wanting me to be happy." No pair of expensive designer jeans could make me as happy as my mom did that day.

The next day, all the girls were wearing their dark denim designer jeans again, but I didn't care. I had on my one-of-a-kind red denim jeans, and I wore them proudly. Most of the girls were again talking about their outfits and where they got their jeans, but two girls told me that they really liked mine and asked where I got them. I told them that no one else in the world could have a pair like mine, as they were one of a kind. But to be honest, even if nobody had complimented me on my jeans that day, it wouldn't have mattered. I looked different, I felt special, and even more importantly, I felt loved by the greatest mother in the world. It doesn't get any better than that.

Helpful Vocabulary Words and Discussion Questions for "Not Like Everybody Else"

Vocabulary words: beaming, glittery, hem, uniform, designer, commercials, expensive, compliment, troubling, budget, individuality, unique, assumption, demeanor, routine, receive, squeal, radar, slight, value

Discussion Questions

1. Why did Patti's classmates' lack of reaction to her outfit affect her confidence on the first Dress Down Day but not on the next one?

2. Should we allow other people's reactions to our taste in clothes, music, food, or anything else we like affect us? Why or why not?

3. Why do you suppose people want to fit in with their crowd rather than be their unique selves?

STORY 14
Being a Person of Excellence

I will never forget what my dad said to me as we were sitting in the car one day. "Antonia, there are teachers everywhere who show us wonderful examples of what to do and what not to do. I want you to be a great example to others, to be a person of excellence."

When he first said that to me — "a person of excellence" — I was confused. I wondered if he wanted me to be perfect in every way. I was pretty sure that wasn't going to happen, especially if anyone looked at my grades in science class. But he patiently explained that being a person of excellence did not mean trying to be perfect but striving to do the right thing and be your best. "Nobody is perfect, but if you live your life with integrity, you can always be proud of yourself."

The phrase "person of excellence" was new to me, but the concept wasn't. My parents always taught my brother and me to be honest and do the right thing. We were witnesses to the way they lived their lives, so I knew this phrase was true for them and wasn't an arbitrary line they were feeding us. My dad regularly pointed out examples of people being excellent to make sure I knew what he meant.

"Take a look at that lady over there who just finished emptying her shopping cart. Do you see how she is returning the cart all the way back to the front of the store despite the fact that it's raining heavily? She is being a person of excellence. Many people leave the carts in the parking area, where they end up damaging

people's cars or blocking empty parking spaces. It also makes it more difficult for the employees who must return the carts to the store. By putting the cart back where it belongs, she is showing consideration for others."

"Daddy, I know; you're always telling us to put things back where we found them."

As Dad pulled out of our parking space, he said, "Yes, Antonia, because if you don't do it, you create more work for someone who was not responsible for moving it in the first place."

Most of the time I found it pretty easy to be a person of excellence. Sometimes it took a little more effort, but one time something happened that proved to be very challenging for me.

One Monday afternoon, my teacher announced that our class was going to have an election to choose a student representative. The representative would meet with the fourth-grade teachers and the school's principal to help organize events for the class, including field trips. The class was thrilled with the idea that they could be involved in making these decisions, and I was excited at the thought of taking this leadership role to help my class. I was a little hesitant because I knew I wasn't the most popular student in the class, but I decided to run anyway.

The following day our teacher asked who was interested in running, and I was one of three who raised their hands. All the students were excited about the upcoming election; it was all anyone could talk about at lunchtime that day.

Two days before the election, one of my classmates, Danielle, pulled me aside and told me some startling information. She said she thought that Molly, one of the girls running for representative, had cheated during a science test. She hadn't said anything to the teacher, but she thought I should confront Molly about it to get her to drop out of the race, or else tell the teacher.

She said, "With her out of the competition, you'll have a much better chance of winning, Antonia. I'm only telling you because I like you more than I like her, and I think you would do a better job. Besides, who wants a cheater to be our representative?" I was shocked and speechless and didn't know what to do. "I'll think about it," I said.

I did just that, and in fact, it was all I could think about. I really wanted to win the election, and if Molly was eliminated, I would have a better chance. But I wasn't sure if the information was true or just a mean rumor. If she had cheated, she probably wouldn't admit to it anyway. If she denied it and I told the teacher, I could get her in trouble for something she might not have done. I didn't know what to do. My dad's words came back to me: "Always be a person of excellence." Then I knew just what to do.

104 BEING YOUR BEST AND NOT COMPARING YOURSELF TO OTHERS

The next day Danielle pulled me aside and asked, "Antonia, have you decided? Are you going to confront Molly or tell the teacher?" I told her I wasn't going to do anything. "While I'd really like to win," I explained, "I'd rather participate in this election fairly and with a clear conscience."

The election was held the next day, and I was really happy with the speech I made. It was a tight race, but Molly ended up winning by two votes. Although I was disappointed, I congratulated her and wished her luck.

I never did find out if Molly cheated on that science test, but she ended up doing a good job as our class representative. When I look back on that moment, I'm pleased with the decision I made, even if I didn't win the election.

Doing the right thing is not always easy, and things may not always work out the way we want. When we try to be a person of excellence, though, we can always look in the mirror and be proud of the reflection looking back at us. That will always be good enough for me.

Helpful Vocabulary Words and Discussion Questions for "A Person of Excellence"

Vocabulary words: phrase, integrity, concept, witnesses, arbitrary, damaging, eliminate, election, representative, involved, leadership, upcoming, regularly, startling, confront, speechless, rumor, reflection, patiently, strive

Discussion Questions

1. At the end of the story, Antonia says she is happy with her decision, even though she didn't end up winning the election. Why do you think she felt that way?

2. Why do you think Danielle was pressuring Antonia to confront Molly or else inform the teacher about her suspicions instead of doing it herself?

3. Antonia said "Doing the right thing isn't always easy." Have you ever been faced with a choice in which doing the right thing was very challenging?

PART VI
Coping with Disappointment, Envy, and Preconceived Views

STORY 15
Eleni's Disappointment

"Where is it? Where did I put it? Mom, I can't find the new sunscreen we bought!" I yelled from my bedroom.

"I already packed the sunscreen, Eleni," Mom answered from downstairs. "Are you almost done packing?"

"Yes, I'm finally ready."

I could barely endure my enthusiasm because the next day we were going on our vacation. We had been meticulously planning this trip to Disney World for months. We mapped out all the attractions we would visit, and in what order. I had seen pictures and videos of these places, but after our flight, we would actually be there.

"Eleni, we need to go to bed very early tonight because our flight leaves at nine in the morning," Mom said.

"Mom, I'll go to bed early, but I doubt I'll sleep much from all my excitement."

The phone rang, and while I could not hear the entire conversation, I quickly realized that something terrible had happened. My mom grew pale and was noticeably upset. When she hung up, she said, "Grab your jacket and shoes, Eleni. We're heading to the hospital. Grandma fell down." She had slipped on some ice outside her house. Luckily, one of her neighbors saw it happen and came to help her. The ambulance had taken her to the emergency room.

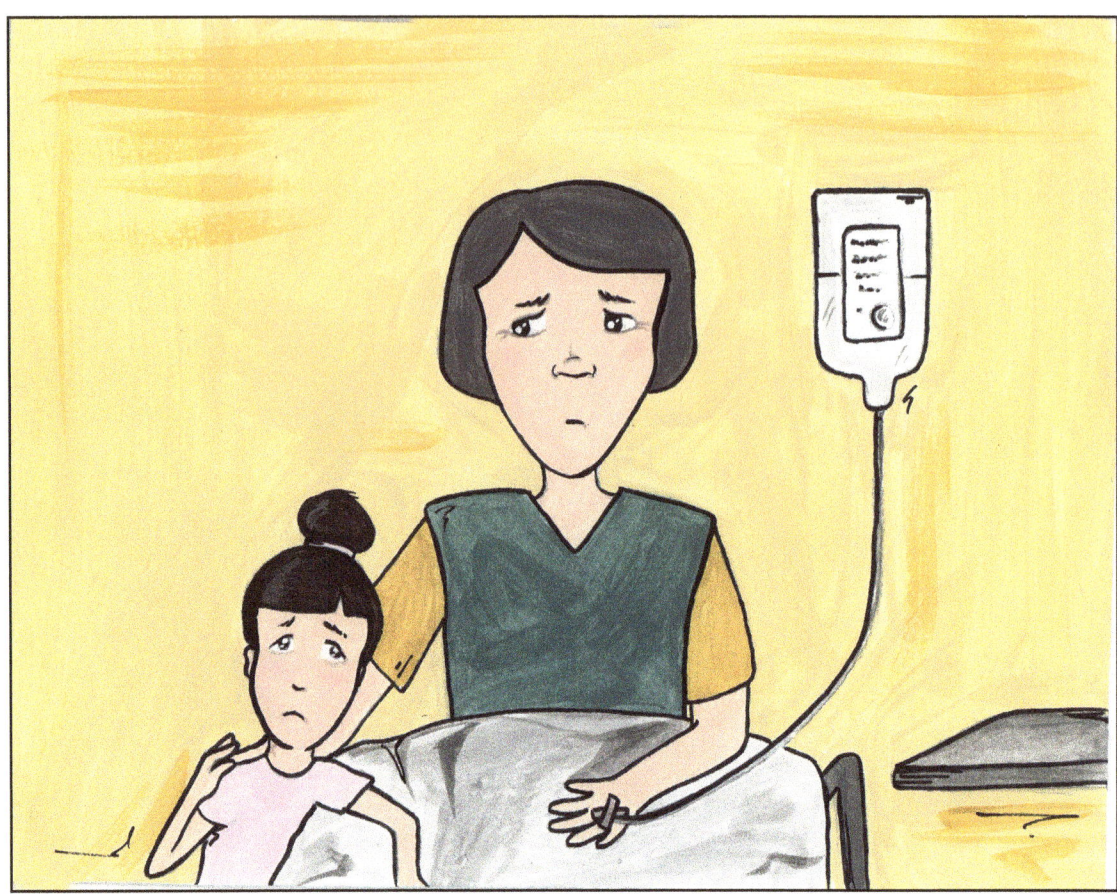

We arrived at the hospital, where we waited for many hours. I was able to see Grandma for a few moments, but it was shocking and heartbreaking to see her lying in bed in so much pain. She had always led an active lifestyle, and she even taught adult dance classes three times a week.

My mom's friend Debbie came by the hospital to visit Grandma, and then took me home with her. She and Mom didn't want me to stay in the emergency room waiting area all night. As I lay in Debbie's extra bedroom that night, I wondered if Grandma was going to be okay and if we would still make our flight in time.

My mom came over to Debbie's house early the next morning to pick me up. She looked exhausted and drained, as she had gotten only a few hours of sleep. I hugged her and asked, "Mommy, how's Grandma?"

My mom took my hands in hers and said, "She's feeling better, but she's still in the hospital. Unfortunately, she broke her hip, so she is going to need surgery. It's scheduled for later today. I'm sorry, sweetheart, but we have to cancel our trip."

My heart sank. I felt terrible for Grandma, but honestly, my disappointment was worse. I didn't say anything to my mom at that time because I knew she was worried about Grandma, but inside my head, a little voice was screaming, "Why did this have to happen now? It's not fair!"

I asked, "Since she's having the surgery today, do you think maybe we could go to Disney World tomorrow or the day after instead?"

"Eleni, I'm sorry," she answered, "but Grandma is going to need our help for many weeks. I just don't know when we'll be able to go. Right now, I'm going to use my vacation days from work to help her. Once she is released from the hospital, she will stay with us for a while. It could be for a month or two."

I was silent, and I didn't say a word the whole way home, either. Mom told me to take a shower and pack my toothbrush, pajamas, and a change of clothes because I was going to spend the rest of the day and that night at Debbie's again.

"Why can't I at least come to the hospital, Mom?" I whimpered. "I love Debbie, but I want to be with you and Grandma."

"Eleni, sweetheart, you can come visit once she's feeling better. Don't worry, you'll have plenty of time with her after she comes home."

I've always loved spending time with Debbie, but now I was too disappointed and upset to enjoy myself. I just wanted to sulk and wallow in pity. I kept thinking, *Why did this have to happen to Grandma, and why now?*

Debbie was trying hard to change my mood. She suggested going shopping or to the movies, but I didn't want to do any of that. This was not the way I had planned to spend my week off from school. All I could think about for the past month was this vacation, and now it was cancelled. I was also very worried about Grandma. What if she wouldn't be able to walk again?

Mom called a few hours later and let us know that Grandma's surgery was a success and that she was resting. I was so relieved. I asked, "Can she walk now? Can I speak to her?" Mom said, "Both of those will happen in time, sweetheart, but not yet."

I was thankful Grandma's surgery was a success, but I was still feeling depressed. I thought Mom and I would be having so much fun together this week, but now I barely even saw her. Debbie took me to my favorite pizza place and then to the arcade in the hope of cheering me up. She was trying her best to make me smile, and while I appreciated it, I was just too depressed.

Mom came over to have dinner with us, and I could see how exhausted she was feeling. She had dark circles under her eyes and didn't even have enough energy to drive home after we ate. Instead, she stayed over at Debbie's and shared the spare bedroom with me.

"Eleni, tomorrow you can come with me to visit Grandma in the hospital," she said. "I'm sure she will be happy to see you."

"Okay, Mom. I can't wait to see her, too," I replied. But she had already fallen asleep.

The next morning, I went to visit Grandma in her hospital room, happy to see her feeling better. Mom and a nurse helped her get out of bed and sit in a chair, but she couldn't walk more than a few steps. Then Mom went down to the cafeteria to get us a snack and drink while I kept Grandma company.

"Having you here with me is the best medicine of all, Eleni. I feel so much better having you and your mom around. I'm very sorry you didn't get to go on your vacation. I didn't want to ruin your plans, but I must admit, I would have felt much worse if you weren't here."

I grabbed her hands, smiled, and said, "I love you, Grandma, and I'm glad I'm here." I realized then that it was much more important to help Grandma feel better than to complain about missing a trip. After all, what she was going through was more difficult than dealing with the disappointment of a cancelled vacation.

When Mom came back, she and the nurse helped Grandma get to the bathroom. The nurse stepped out for a moment to go get Grandma her medicine. When she returned, she told me, "Your mom is quite a special lady, sweetheart. Your grandmother told me you two were supposed to be on vacation now. Not many people would sacrifice their vacation time to take care of somebody else and do it without complaint. She's quite the hero." She went back to the bathroom to help Mom bring Grandma back to her bed.

She was right. My mom hadn't complained once. She had been running back and forth to the hospital, meeting with doctors, taking care of Grandma, and making sure I was taken care of, and she had never said anything about missing her vacation time. All this time I had been sulking and feeling sorry for myself;

she had more reason to complain than I did, yet she never did. She had shown grace and strength during this difficult time. I smiled with pride as I thought about how lucky I was to have such an amazing mother.

Grandma was released from the hospital a few days later, and we brought her home with us. Mom and I helped her while she recovered, and eventually, after several months of physical therapy, she was back to her old self. She even started teaching her dance class again.

As luck would have it, a year later Grandma won four tickets to Disney World in a church raffle, and we finally got to take our vacation. Grandma and Debbie came with Mom and me, and we had an incredible time. I knew that the trip ended up being better than if we had gone without them. Mom said, "Sometimes our plans don't go the way we expected, but if we keep a good attitude, the future might surprise us with something even better."

I try to remember those wise words and that memorable trip every time I face a disappointment. It helps me to smile again and be hopeful that something better lies ahead.

Helpful Vocabulary Words and Discussion Questions for "Eleni's Disappointment"

Vocabulary words: disappointment, enthusiasm, meticulous, attractions, pale, doubt, heartbreaking, lifestyle, exhausted, drained, noticeable, pity, release, depressed, complaint, sacrifice, whimper, recover, physical therapy, sulk

Discussion Questions

1. Eleni was extremely disappointed when her vacation had to be cancelled. What was the turning point that helped her move past her feelings of self-pity?

2. What lessons did Eleni learn as a result of her grandmother's accident?

3. If you have ever suffered a big disappointment, how did you handle it? Did it teach you anything about yourself?

STORY 16
Tommy's Bike

"Blow out your candles and make a wish," Tommy's mother said. Tommy blew them out with one big breath. He knew in his heart what he wanted for his birthday, as he had been longing for and working toward his goal for some time: a bike.

Tommy had been saving whatever money he could for the past two years. Some of his savings was from birthday and holiday gifts, and the rest was money he earned raking leaves for the neighbors in the fall, shoveling snow for them in the winter, and cutting their grass in the spring and summer. Although he was just turning eleven, Tommy was a hard-working and responsible boy. *If I get twenty dollars for my birthday, I will have enough for that bike to finally be mine*, he thought.

After enjoying the delicious birthday cake his sisters and mother had made, he opened his gifts. His best friend, David, got him a board game, his two older sisters got him a sweater and a pair of jeans, and his grandparents gave him a series of books he really wanted to read. When he opened the birthday card his parents gave him, he was stunned to find fifty dollars inside. "Now, son," his dad said, "you'll finally be able to get the bike you've had your heart set on. Mom and I will take you to the bicycle shop tomorrow, and we'll pick it up."

Tommy couldn't contain his excitement and squealed with joy. After all this time, the bike he wanted so dearly would finally be his. David was excited for his friend, too, because Tommy always told him that he would let him ride his bike when he got it. Even though David had a bike of his own, the one Tommy had his heart set on was pretty special. It could go faster than most and was great for riding up hills. David knew they would have an awesome time riding their bikes together.

When they first met, David had wondered why Tommy's parents had not bought the bike for him, as he knew that his family had the means to do so. He asked Tommy about it once, soon after they became friends.

"Well," Tommy had said, "I used to have a very nice bike that my parents had bought for me. I loved that bike and used to ride it all the time. But the truth is, I was irresponsible with it. Once I left it in our driveway right underneath the car, and my dad almost ran over it.

"Then one day I really messed up. My mom kept telling me to bring the bike back into the garage, but I left it outside, and it was stolen. I was so upset, and my parents were really mad at me. They told me that if I had paid for the bike myself, I would have been more careful with it. They told me they were not going to buy me another bike and that if I wanted a new one, I'd have to earn it, so ever since then, I've been doing lots of odd jobs for our neighbors to save enough money to buy a new bike."

The next day, as promised, Tommy's parents took him to the bike shop, and he bought his new bike. He even had thirty dollars left over. His parents bought him a new helmet and a chain with a lock so he could keep his new bike from being stolen. They told him to save the extra money. Tommy hugged them tightly and thanked them over and over again. He said, "Mom, Dad, I promise that I will be careful with this bike and never take it for granted. I know exactly what you meant when you told me that I'd be more responsible if I paid for it myself. I know how long and hard I had to work to get this. It wasn't easy, but I feel proud of myself." His mom hugged him and said, "Your father and I are proud of you too, Tommy."

As soon as they got home, Tommy showed his sisters his new bike, and then took it out for his first ride, which was sweeter than he had ever imagined it could be. His first stop was David's house. David was happy for Tommy and marveled at how shiny and new the bike looked. The two of them rode around the neighborhood for over an hour, then they stopped to get something to drink. Tommy couldn't stop smiling the entire day. That night, he carefully cleaned his bike and put it in the garage. As he lay in his bed that night, he couldn't stop thinking about his new bike and how thankful he was to own it.

Every day for the next two weeks, Tommy would rush home after school and take his bike out for a quick ride before starting his homework. He was cautious to not scrape it or lay it down on the sidewalk. Every day he would clean it well and secure it in the garage. The school year was ending, and with the summer vacation approaching, he was excited about having even more fun and more bike rides.

Mark, a classmate of Tommy and David's, was having a party at his house on the last day of school and invited all of his fellow students. Tommy and David decided to ride their bikes to Mark's house, as it was only three blocks away. The boys put their bikes in Mark's backyard and locked them to a fence. Tommy wasn't taking any chances of having his bike stolen again.

The boys had a great time at the party. They ate pizza and snacks, listened to music, danced, and played video games. At six o'clock, the party was coming to an end, and it was time for Tommy and David to leave.

When they went to get their bikes, they were horrified to see that someone had vandalized Tommy's new bike. They had slashed the tires and seat, and the front fender was bent. Tommy screamed, "My bike, my bike!" as he fell to the ground and wept. David tried to console him but was so shocked and upset himself that he couldn't find the words. There wasn't anything anyone could say to Tommy to make him feel better.

Mark, his parents, and the kids who were still at the party came out. They all were shocked by what had happened—especially right in the backyard. David's bike had not been vandalized, and neither had two other bikes that were nearby. Everyone was saying, "Who would do such a thing? Why would anyone do something so cruel? Why did they do this to poor Tommy?"

Tommy was speechless. His heart sank. All he could think was, *Two years of hard work and saving my money, destroyed in a moment. Why?*

Mark's parents felt very bad. They called Tommy's parents and told them what had happened, and Tommy's dad came over right away. Mark's parents offered to pay for the repairs because the vandalism had taken place in their backyard. Tommy's dad thanked them for the offer but told them he would take care of it. He hugged Tommy and said, "Don't worry, son, I'll make sure your bike will be repaired as good as new." Although that made Tommy feel a little better, he was still awfully depressed. "Thanks, Dad," he glumly said.

As they rode in the car, Tommy asked, "Dad, what makes somebody do something so mean?" His dad said, "Son, I don't know. It's hard to understand what motivates a person to destroy another's property. Sometimes people just make terrible choices and don't think about who they might hurt."

Tommy's bike was at the repair shop for a few days, but soon he was out riding it and enjoying himself again. A few weeks later, while he was at the park, David overheard a conversation on the basketball court between one of his classmates, Mario, and Mario's brother. Mario was bragging that he was the one who destroyed Tommy's bike. His brother was surprised and asked him why he had done it.

Mario said, "Well, who did he think he was showing up with that fancy-schmancy expensive bike? He was doing it to make us feel bad because we don't have expensive bikes. He just did it to show off. He's not any better than the rest of us, so I just decided to make him feel bad, too."

David angrily approached Mario and erupted. "You did that?! Do you have any idea how long and hard Tommy worked to get that bike? He worked and saved his money for two years to buy it himself. If you were willing to work as hard and save your money for that long, maybe you could get one yourself. How would you feel if that was done to you after you worked and saved for so long to get it?"

Mario said, "So what! I don't care how long it took him. He was still just trying to show off and make all of us feel bad for not having a bike like that. And if you tell anyone that I did it, I'll just deny it. You can't prove anything. Nobody will believe you, and my brother won't tell on me, either."

David left the park and rushed over to Tommy's house to tell him and his parents what he had overheard. Tommy was shocked because he had known Mario for years, and it wasn't in his character to be so mean.

"Well, Tommy," his dad said, "now we know why your bike was vandalized: envy. It's unfortunate that Mario didn't handle his feelings better and made a poor choice."

Tommy shook his head, still in shock over learning the truth. "I don't understand. If he wanted a bike like mine, he could have saved up his money and bought one, too. Why did he have to ruin mine?"

David said, "I guess he figured if he couldn't have one right now, nobody else should."

"Dad, what do we do now?" asked Tommy. "How can we prove he did this?"

"Unfortunately, we can't, Tommy. I know you might find that frustrating, but you need to let go of the anger you feel, because it won't change anything, it will only upset you more. You should try to forgive him and hope that in time he will come to regret his choice and see how it affected others — and himself."

"But Dad, if he gets away with it, it won't affect him."

"Son, the choices we make always have consequences, good or bad. Even if you never see how this will affect him, it doesn't mean it won't. He may already be feeling terrible guilt or embarrassment. Besides, your mom and I are grateful that the only thing damaged was the bike, and it's been fixed."

Tommy was still upset, but he knew that his dad was right. Why hold on to the anger and ruin the rest of his summer? He made the decision to let it go and just enjoy himself.

Weeks later, when the new school year started, Tommy came face to face with Mario. Mario thought for sure that Tommy would yell at him about what he did to the bike; he had already planned what he would say in his defense. Instead, Tommy went up to him and said, "If you ever want to take my bike for a ride, you can."

Mario was at a loss for words. Why was Tommy being nice to him, especially when he knew what he had done? Then he muttered, "I'm sorry."

Mario never did ask Tommy to ride his bike. Maybe he was too embarrassed or remorseful about what he had done. As for Tommy, he continued to work after school to save up for the next thing he wanted to get: a car for his eighteenth birthday.

Helpful Vocabulary Words and Discussion Questions for "Tommy's Bike"

Vocabulary words: means, marvel, cautious, secure, horrified, vandalize, slash, fender, wept, console, glum, erupt, deny, envy, consequences, mutter, remorse, irresponsible, awesome, embarrass

Discussion Questions

1. Why was Tommy's attitude toward his new bike different from his attitude about the bike that had been stolen a couple of years earlier?

2. Why do you think Tommy offered to let Mario ride his bike?

3. Tommy's behavior is an example of forgiveness and compassion toward somebody who hurt him. Can you share about a time that you needed someone to forgive you for a mistake you made? How did it feel to be forgiven? Have you ever forgiven someone who hurt you? What helped you forgive them?

STORY 17
Tuning In to Your Truth

"Hey kiddo, how was your day?" I heard his voice, and before I even saw his face, I knew it was my Uncle Steve. "Uncle Steve, I didn't know you were coming to pick me up from practice today," I said, grinning with joy from ear to ear. He had that effect on everyone; you always felt happy whenever he was around.

"Well, Charlie, I went by to visit your mom, and she told me she was coming to pick you up from practice. I asked her to let me come get you instead so we could have some one-on-one time," he said as he gave me a big hug. I was just thrilled because I always enjoyed spending time with Uncle Steve. Even if we were doing something that I would ordinarily find boring, he had a way of making it fun.

He was renovating an apartment in a building he owned and had to select some floor tiles to give the carpenter, so he asked if I would mind going with him and helping him choose the tiles. I didn't mind at all, and I was really touched that he wanted my input on the decision.

After we picked out the tiles, we loaded them into his car and headed home. I was so comfortable with Uncle Steve that it was easy for me to share what was on my mind, and I wanted to tell him what had happened at band practice that day.

"Uncle Steve, do you mind if I ask you something?"

"Not at all, kiddo. What's on your mind?"

"Every year the school band takes part in competitions with other local schools, and then those winners compete with other winners throughout the state. This year, our band won first place at the local level, and now we will be competing against Watercrest Middle School, the school I used to go to before we moved here last year. I used to play with their band, and I'm still very close to my friends there. But today, a few members of the band at my new school had some really unflattering things to say about the Watercrest band kids."

"So, what did you do?" asked Uncle Steve.

"Well," I answered sheepishly, "I was kind of caught off guard. I wanted to say something, but I didn't. What do you think I should do?"

He nodded his head and said, "Well, you are a smart young man, Charlie, and I know you'll figure out what to do if the situation comes up again, which it probably will."

I had wanted to ask Uncle Steve about this because he's one of the smartest people I know, and I really wanted him to tell me what to do instead of trusting me to figure it out. I blocked it out of my mind, but that night it wandered back in just as I was trying to sleep. I shrugged it off and told myself that maybe it wouldn't come up again. I rolled over onto my side and fell asleep.

The next day was pretty normal, and as I had hoped the night before, nothing about the Watercrest band kids came up again, so I was happy. It had taken me quite a while to make friends at this new school, and the majority of them were in the band. I didn't want anything to get in the way of my new friendships.

The day after that was even better. Since it was Friday, some of my bandmates and I went out for pizza after practice. We had a wonderful time, and I decided that I had gotten all upset the other day for nothing. I could just relax and enjoy myself.

My family and Uncle Steve's family always went over to Grandma's house on Sundays for our weekly family dinner. We all brought food, but Grandma would always prepare the main dish. My cousins, my sister, and I would play some games, and the adults would join us later to watch a movie.

At one point, when I was alone, Uncle Steve asked me how things were going with my bandmates. "There's nothing to worry about, Uncle Steve," I answered. "It's never come up again, so it's all over."

"Have you given any thought to what you might do if the situation does come up again, Charlie?" he asked.

"Not really," I answered. "I don't want to think about it, because it may never come up."

"Okay," he answered, grinning as if he had a secret I knew nothing about.

A few days later, during practice, our band teacher was talking about the upcoming competition that Sunday. He said it was important that we feel confident, as the competition was going to be fierce. This subsequently led to a conversation about the kids at Watercrest Middle School. I suddenly had a sinking feeling in my stomach.

As everyone was getting ready to leave school, Larry, who was the senior member of the band, began telling a story of a kid from Watercrest who was once caught cheating on a high school entrance exam. He said, "All the kids who go to Watercrest are cheaters. It's a known fact. I'll bet they will try to cheat at the competition, too." The other kids were shocked by this news.

I was upset and getting sicker by the minute. I guess nobody knew that I had transferred from Watercrest. How would they feel about me if they knew I was from there? But I wasn't a cheat, and none of my friends at Watercrest were cheaters, either. I really wanted to speak up but was afraid to. Then a girl named Stella asked, "How could they possibly cheat in the competition?" The other kids began thinking it over and started asking the same thing.

"They might try to sabotage our band or the results somehow," said Maureen, who played trombone.

"That wouldn't be easy, but you never know what experienced cheaters might do. They can't be trusted, so we have to expect anything," said Larry. I just stood silent, feeling nervous and unprepared to defend my friends and my old school.

As fate would have it, when I got home, Uncle Steve was there. He could tell by the way I hugged him that something was troubling me. He followed me into my room and asked, "What's bothering you, kiddo? How are things going at band practice?"

"Is it that obvious?" I asked him.

"Let's just say I have a little experience reading people's moods, especially yours," he answered. "Did somebody bring up the Watercrest kids again?"

"Yes, they did," I answered glumly.

"Well, how did you handle it this time?"

"I didn't. I just stood there silent again, afraid that they might think less of me if they knew I transferred from there. One guy called all the kids from Watercrest cheaters, because he said a kid once cheated on an exam. That doesn't mean everyone in the school is a cheater. Even though I know they're not, I didn't defend my friends or the school at all, and now I feel bad," I answered.

"Well, Charlie," Uncle Steve explained, "many times people pass judgment on an entire group based on one or two people's poor choices. Unfortunately, this happens often, and it often leads to the false labeling of an entire group. Now, in this situation, you are in a position where you can perpetuate this false judgment

by keeping your silence so you don't risk losing your new friends, or you can be honest, defend your friends at Watercrest, and defend yourself as a former student."

"What if I tell the truth and then they don't want to be my friends anymore?"

"That may very well happen," he said. "The choice is ultimately yours. While at first neither choice feels easy or comfortable in a situation like this, I usually choose the one I will be proud of in the long run." This is why I love talking to Uncle Steve. He always knows just the right advice to give me.

The competition was a day and a half away, and I was more worried about my dilemma than the competition because I still didn't know what I should do. I knew all my old friends would be there on Sunday because they had messaged me to say how excited they were to see me again. I was really looking forward to seeing them, too, and catching up afterward. I couldn't just ignore them; I would be crushed if they did that to me.

I finally made my decision. On Sunday morning, before our last practice, I asked the band teacher if I could make an announcement. I told all of the band members that I had transferred from Watercrest, and that most of its band members were friends of mine. I told them that I didn't want them to be surprised if they saw me talking to them and that I regretted not saying something about it sooner. I admitted that I had been afraid that I might jeopardize my new friendships.

Larry said, "So that's how they planned on cheating in this competition—they put a spy on our team! You were pretending to be our friend all this time. That's why you kept it a secret!" The kids started whispering among themselves. *Is it true? Is he a spy? What do you think he told them?*

The band teacher said, "That's enough, Larry, and the rest of you. Charlie is not a spy. I've always known he transferred from Watercrest. They are a fine band, and they don't need to cheat. I've known their band teacher from when we were in band together at Watercrest many years ago." The other students were even more shocked at this announcement than Charlie was.

The band teacher continued, "It took Charlie a lot of courage to be honest with you about having friends on the opposition. Being on opposing teams doesn't mean we must criticize or vilify the other team. We should just do our best, and hopefully our best will be better than theirs. But if not, we will go over and congratulate them on a job well done."

I could see that Larry and his best friend were still a little suspicious of me, but my other bandmates rallied around me. Having been honest with them, I felt like a weight that had been sitting on my shoulders was suddenly lifted. I finally found peace, and I played the best I ever had at the competition. Afterward, as I sat between my new friends and old friends waiting for the results, I realized that regardless of what the results were that day, I was already a winner.

Helpful Vocabulary Words and Discussion Questions for "Tuning In to Your Truth"

Vocabulary words: unflattering, renovate, input, subsequently, regardless, unprepared, jeopardize, judgment, label, perpetuate, dilemma, opposition, vilify, suspicious, rallied, criticize, grinning, off guard, sabotage, sheepish

Discussion Questions

1. Charlie was nervous that his new bandmates might not accept him if they knew he had transferred from Watercrest. If you have ever been nervous about sharing something with a group for fear of being rejected, how did you handle it?

2. During a band practice, Larry said a student was caught cheating at Watercrest and concluded that all of the students at that school were cheaters. Why was this a terrible statement to make?

3. What did Charlie mean when he said, "Regardless of what the results were that day, I was already a winner"?

PART VII
Kindness and Compassion

STORY 18
Penny's Surprise

Little Penny sat in her room impatiently waiting for her mom to get dressed. It was Saturday, the day that this five-year old and her mother did their weekly shopping and errands. She always enjoyed spending this time with her mom and then having lunch together. "I'm ready!" her mom called, and out their door they went.

As they were leaving, Penny encountered Mr. Joe, the mail carrier. She nervously tugged at her mom's jacket and clung to her. Mr. Joe usually wore a scowl on his face, and today was no exception. Penny was frightened by his expression, but it didn't seem to bother her mom, who stopped and spoke with him.

When her mom first greeted Mr. Joe, his mood seemed unchanged, but the more she spoke with him, the more his face softened. She asked him about his family and specifically his wife, having heard from a neighbor that she was ill. Mr. Joe seemed different now. He wasn't grumpy any more, and Penny stopped clinging to her mom. Her mom told Mr. Joe that she would keep his family in her thoughts and wished him a wonderful day. A huge smile filled his face, and his eyes conveyed his thanks.

Penny was amazed. "Mom," she asked, "How did you do that? He never smiles. Weren't you afraid to talk to him?"

"No," her mom answered. "He's a person like you and me. Sometimes people who seem unhappy or mean are just feeling sad or lonely. I wanted him to know that somebody cares about him and the difficulties he is facing. A little kindness can go a long way. Sometimes you can brighten a person's day by giving them a simple smile. Always remember, Penny, kindness is contagious."

Penny looked confused. "Mom, isn't contagious when you have chicken pox?"

Her mom chuckled and explained, "Sweetheart, chicken pox is contagious, too, but in a different way. 'Contagious' means that something spreads easily from person to person. So, if you do something nice for somebody and it puts them in a good mood, they might end up doing something nice for someone else."

Penny's face lit up. "Oh, I get it. So now Mr. Joe might do something nice for somebody else, too!"

"Yes," said her mom, "that could happen."

"Mom," said Penny, "I'm glad you're my mommy and that you made Mr. Joe feel better. I'm going to do nice things for other people today just like you did."

"That's wonderful," said her mother. "I'm always very proud when you do nice things for others, like when you helped your dad and me put the groceries away yesterday."

Penny grabbed her mom's hand and smiled. She was proud of her mom, too. Just witnessing her being kind to Mr. Joe made her feel wonderful.

They climbed into the car, and off they went. Their first stop was the dry-cleaning store. Penny liked going there because Mr. and Mrs. Kagan, the owners, were always nice to her. They always offered her a piece of strawberry candy from the bowl next to the cash register. Mr. Kagan would pinch her cheeks and tell her she was the cutest five-year-old customer he ever had. Penny suddenly understood why she always felt so wonderful after visiting their store: it was because they always showed her kindness.

As they were leaving, Penny noticed a woman struggling to push her baby's carriage through the door. She dashed over and said, "Please let me help you." She held the door open for the woman, just as she did for her classmates in school. The grateful woman smiled and said, "Thank you. I've had so much difficulty with this carriage today. That's the nicest thing that's happened to me all morning." Penny realized in that moment that doing kind things for others made her feel wonderful, and she decided to continue doing good deeds whenever possible.

Penny and her mom were off to their next stop, the bakery. They needed to buy a loaf of bread and some cookies for dessert that night. The store was very busy, and they waited in line to be served. Just as the gentleman in front of them had finished paying for his purchases, Penny noticed that he dropped his wallet while attempting to put it in his back pocket. He was in such a hurry that he hadn't even noticed.

She tapped the man gently on the hand and said, "Excuse me, sir, but you dropped your wallet." The gentleman looked down and said, "Thank you, young lady. I was in such a rush to get back to work, I hadn't even noticed." He looked Penny's mom and said, "What a fine young lady you have here. Her honesty and kindness are admirable." Her face beamed with pride.

138 KINDNESS AND COMPASSION

When the young man working behind the counter saw what Penny did, he decided her behavior deserved a reward, so he reached over and handed her a big, yellow, star-shaped cookie. Penny was ecstatic and thanked the young man. She was about to take a huge bite of her cookie but then decided to save it for later and share it with her mom and dad.

It was time for lunch, so they went to Rocco's Pizzeria because Penny thought they had the best pizza in the world. As Penny began to gobble down her slice, she thought about the nice things she had done and of how wonderfully proud both she and her mom felt because of them. Penny now saw that her mom was showing kindness by bringing her to the pizzeria every Saturday. She wondered how many times she had actually thanked her mom for that. She wasn't sure, but she was determined to show her mom her appreciation that day.

Once they finished eating, Penny threw away the garbage, returned the tray back to the counter, and ran back to hug her mother. She said, "Mommy, thank you for always buying me pizza on Saturdays." Surprised, her mom smiled, and her face lit up. "You're welcome, sweetheart. It's my pleasure."

A little while after they got home, Penny's dad arrived and came into her room. Penny was happier than usual to see him because she couldn't wait to tell him about the day's events and about getting the star cookie. Dad had some news to share, as well, but waited for Penny to tell him her news first.

After Penny told him about her wonderful day and how good she felt helping others, he shared his exciting news with her. That afternoon, he had gone out shopping to buy a new camera to have for Penny's birthday the following week. Their old camera wasn't working well anymore, and he wanted to make sure he would be able to take lots of photos at her birthday party.

The man at the electronics store had showed him different models, and he was trying to decide which one to buy. When he mentioned that he was buying the camera for his daughter's sixth birthday party, the gentleman smiled and said, "You have a little girl at home who's turning six next week? I'll tell you what, take this model. I think it's the best camera we have, and for you, it's on the house."

Penny's dad was confused. Puzzled, he asked, "Why are you giving me a free camera? You don't even know my daughter or me."

The man explained that earlier that day, a little girl had seen him drop his wallet in a bakery and had returned it to him. Her honesty and kindness saved him the inconvenience and trouble of replacing everything in his wallet. He added that her polite manner made an impression on him and put him in a great mood for the rest of the day. Unfortunately, he had had to rush back to his store and hadn't had the chance to properly express his gratitude to the little girl. "So," the gentleman said, "I decided I could do something nice and share some of the kindness that little girl showed me with another little girl."

As her dad finished the story, Penny's eyes widened. "That was me, Dad! That was me! Mom was right. Kindness is contagious like chicken pox and comes back to you. She was right!"

Penny's dad laughed. He couldn't believe the coincidence of it all. He hugged his daughter and said, "I'm so proud of you, Penny, and I'm glad you learned such an important lesson about how powerful kindness can be." Penny was thrilled; her dad's words meant more to her than the new camera ever could. She ran off to share the news with her mom.

The following week was Penny's birthday. She had a wonderful time because her whole family was over to share in this special occasion. They snapped many pictures, and each time Penny saw the new camera, she remembered what a little bit of kindness had done.

As she watched her mom bring out her birthday cake, she made a promise to herself to keep doing kind things for others — not because she wanted anything in return, but because she wanted to witness how it changed people's lives. She thought about how wonderful it would be if everyone started to do just one kind thing a day. Surely it would change the world. And with that thought, she blew out her birthday candles.

Helpful Vocabulary Words and Discussion Questions for "Penny's Surprise"

Vocabulary words: gratitude, nervous, impression, manner, impatient, errands, tug, cling, soften, contagious, struggle, widen, dash, grateful, admirable, appreciation, inconvenience, coincidence, replace, scowl

Discussion questions

1. What motivated Penny to start doing kind acts for others?
2. How did Penny's kindness affect others? How did it affect her?
3. How do you feel when you show kindness to others? Have you ever witnessed kindness spread to others? Explain.

STORY 19
A Trip to the Senior Home

Brrrring! The school bell rang at eight o'clock. As Ms. Brooks walked into her third grade class, children scattered to their desks with anticipation. The teacher's announcement the day before, about a special upcoming event, motivated them to quiet down much quicker than usual.

Ms. Brooks began to speak. "I see how impatient you are to find out the mysterious location of our next class trip." The kids began to ask questions. "Are we going to another museum?" asked Despina. "No," replied Ms. Brooks. "Are we going to the Statue of Liberty? I love going there," said Kelly. "No," replied the teacher once more. "This trip will be unlike any other we've taken, and it will require some preparation before we go." The children looked puzzled but were curious about the mysterious trip.

Ms. Brooks said, "Our next trip, two weeks from today, will be to King's Senior Home."

"What can we learn there?" asked Nikki. "You always say our trips are supposed to be educational."

"You're absolutely correct, Nikki," replied Ms. Brooks. "And I guarantee that this trip will teach you many unexpected lessons. After the trip we'll discuss what we learned, but for now, we have some work to do."

Ms. Brooks read a story to the children about an older gentleman who lived in a senior home. He had lost most of his memory and his ability to speak. His family visited him weekly, and although he could not talk to them, he recognized them, and he had a smile in his eyes when he saw their faces. Sometimes, on really good days, he would grab their hands.

Nicholas said, "This story reminds me of my great-grandmother. She lives with my grandmother because she can't take care of herself anymore. She doesn't call me by name now because she's forgetful and confused, but she still smiles at me when I visit and talk to her. My mom says, 'Nobody ever really forgets the people they love. Their heart always remembers them, even if their mind doesn't.'"

The next day Ms. Brooks read her class a story about a woman who lived alone and had no family nearby. Luckily, the woman finally made friends with a boy who lived next door, and they would work in the garden together.

"It must be lonely not to have family around," said Timothy. "I remember crying when my older brother, Kenny, left for school and I had no one to play with. Even though my mom was still home with me, I couldn't wait for him to come back. I can't imagine how it would feel to be alone every day."

Ms. Brooks explained that while many people at the senior home have family members nearby who visit, others may not have any. She added that some seniors can speak and move around, but others are not as independent and require assistance. "What is most important to remember, children," said Ms. Brooks, "is that even if seniors can't speak, they can feel. A warm smile, a pat on the hand, and a little kindness can do wonders for a person."

"Do you really think we could make the seniors feel special?" asked Kelly. "We're just kids, and that would be really challenging." Ms. Brooks told the children to never underestimate their ability to affect others.

The class decided to create memoir books to read to the residents of the senior home. They thought that sharing their own memories may help the seniors recall some of their own. They also made a special arts and crafts project to give to them, and practiced singing some songs to perform. The kids became excited for the visit as they continued to prepare for their trip.

The day finally arrived, and the children found themselves standing in a large auditorium at the senior home, where people were beginning to gather. Some of the seniors walked into the room on their own, and others came in aided by walkers or being pushed in wheelchairs.

The children were nervous at first. Many of the seniors were looking at them and smiling; others stared around blankly. The students overheard conversations between some of the residents, who were saying things like, "Oh, look at them!" and "They are so cute."

Ms. Brooks chatted with Ms. Tina, the head director of the senior home, and then she addressed the seniors and introduced the class. She took the children around in small groups and introduced them to some of the residents.

Nicholas called his friend Jimmy over and said, "Let's stick together, because I'm a little bashful with strangers, and I'll feel better if you're around." Jimmy said, "Don't worry. I'll stay with you the whole time. Besides, they seem friendly enough."

Nicholas wasn't the only one who was bashful at first; a few other children were, as well, but the enthusiasm of the seniors made their nervousness vanish. Soon the room was overflowing with conversations, smiles, and laughter.

Later, when the children began to sing, many of the residents joined them. After the performance, everyone applauded, and the children beamed with pride. Some seniors shouted, "How wonderful!" "Terrific! "Bravo! Bravo!"

Ms. Tina told the class that the seniors also love to sing. She led them in a song called "Let Me Call You Sweetheart." Although the students had never heard the song before, they thought it was pretty wonderful. Ms. Brooks knew the words and sang along, and as she did, the children noticed her eyes brimming with tears.

When the children's visit was nearing the end, Ms. Tina brought out some juice and cookies for them. Ms. Brooks thanked everyone at the senior home for their hospitality and kindness and let them know what a wonderful time she and the class had. Many of the seniors called out, "Thank you!" and "We had so much fun!" After they finished their snacks, the children said their final goodbyes. Some of the residents came and gave them warm hugs and asked them to come back for another visit.

Once the students were back in their classroom, they sat together and shared spirited conversations about their experiences with the residents of the senior home. Kelly shared a story about one of the residents she met. "Ms. Beverly was a dancer who did a special type of dance called flamenco. Now, at ninety years old, she can't dance the same way, but she still wiggles around in her wheelchair and waves her arms in the air."

Despina told the class about an elderly gentleman named Mr. Christopher. "He said I reminded him of his daughter because she had hazel eyes and blonde hair when she was little. His daughter and her family live very far away, so he doesn't see them often. He said our visit was the most fun he had had since coming to the senior home a year ago."

Nikki met a man who was a World War II veteran and served our country in Germany. She said, "He told me that although it was a very tough time for him, he was proud to serve his country."

Ms. Brooks's eyes welled up with tears as she told the story of another resident, Ms. Helen. Ms. Helen had been sitting in a wheelchair on the far side of the room, wearing a lovely green shawl. She had not spoken since coming to the senior home two years earlier, but when the students began to sing, she actually started to sing along with them. Ms. Brooks added, "Later, when I complimented her on her shawl, she said I could have it, but I told her she looked too beautiful with it and that she should keep it. Ms. Tina thought this was nothing short of miraculous. Class, I believe your singing worked magic for her. I am so proud of you!"

The children were overjoyed and began to cheer for themselves, filled with a great sense of pride. They couldn't wait to go home and share their stories with their families. At dismissal time, Nikki turned to her teacher and said, "You were right, Ms. Brooks. Today's trip taught me more than any other. I hope we can go back again."

A few days later, the school's principal came by Ms. Brooks's class and read a beautiful letter he had received from Ms. Tina at King's Senior Home. In it, Ms. Tina complimented the class on their wonderful performance as well as their extraordinary behavior and kindness. The principal was delighted and said it was an honor to have such kind and compassionate students in his school. He presented the entire class with a service award to display in their classroom.

Ms. Brooks told the students that she had another surprise for them. She read a letter from a woman who had been visiting her mother at the senior home on the day the children were there. Because the woman lives in another state, she rarely has the opportunity to visit. She was so impressed with the children's kindheartedness that she wanted to express her gratitude to them by sending them packages of jellybeans from the candy factory where she worked.

The class was thrilled, and Despina suggested sending the woman a thank you card. Ms. Brooks wholeheartedly agreed, and the children all enjoyed the jellybeans after lunch. That afternoon, Jimmy said, "Ms. Brooks, even if we hadn't gotten the jellybeans, I'd still be happy that we went on this trip because it made me feel good inside. The jellybeans were just an added bonus."

Ms. Brooks smiled. "Remember, children, any good deed you do will be returned to you, sometimes in ways you can never imagine." The students looked at their teacher and smiled. They would all carry the memories of this trip and the lessons it offered for their lifetimes.

Helpful Vocabulary Words and Discussion Questions for "A Trip to the Senior Home"

Vocabulary words: veteran, scattered, auditorium, memoir, blankly, bashful, brimming, hospitality, shawl, miraculous, compassionate, kindhearted, wholehearted, vanish, spirited, underestimate, overheard, mysterious, preparation, independent

Discussion Questions

1. How did the children's visit affect the residents of the senior home?

2. What do you think was the greatest lesson the students learned after visiting the senior home?

3. If there are seniors in your life you enjoy spending time with, what kinds of things do you enjoy doing together? It could be a grandparent, great-grandparent, great-aunt, great-uncle, or an elderly neighbor or friend.

STORY 20
A Double Test of Patience

It was one of those hot and sticky summer nights that made sitting on the front stoop uncomfortable. Nonetheless, my family gathered outside, as was common practice in the neighborhood, sipping some cool iced tea and discussing the day's events.

Although the air conditioner inside could offer some relief, we preferred to be outdoors and chat with the neighbors, who were also sitting outside. The cold winters of the northeast never afforded this luxury, so my family took full advantage of every opportunity we had to spend time outdoors before the frigid temperatures sneaked their way back in.

I went inside to refill the pitcher of iced tea when I heard my mom shout, "Angelina, is that smoke coming from the Marcuses' house?"

Before I could get to the door to go look, my grandmother rushed into the house to call the fire department. I ran outside and saw my mom and my two older brothers running down the block with two of our neighbors. Luckily, the house was not yet fully ablaze, and they were able to help the family evacuate. The fire department arrived moments later, and the fire was put out before it caused major damage.

But the Marcuses' house was filled with smoke and water, and they would not be able to stay there for at least a few weeks. I wasn't surprised when my mom offered to let the family stay with us until they could arrange for other

accommodations while their house was being repaired. This generosity of spirit was typical of my mom; she was always going out of her way to help people.

Only the kitchen had been affected by the fire, which turned out to be caused by a malfunction of an appliance, and the fire department informed the Marcus family that it was safe to go inside and collect a few things. Mr. and Mrs. Marcus went in to get some clothes while we kept watch over their three-year-old twins.

We had quite the full house that evening. It was pretty crowded and noisy, and there was a rather long wait for the bathroom at times, but we didn't mind; these were not ordinary circumstances. Grandma gave up her room and slept with Mom in her room, and my brothers and I slept on Mom's bedroom floor. My brothers' room and the bedroom I shared with Grandma were given to our guests for the night.

The next morning, I awoke to the sound of feet scampering along the hall and running up and down the stairs. The Marcus twins were up bright and early, checking out their new surroundings. Louie began to cry because he didn't have his favorite stuffed bear. Mr. Marcus told him he would go by their house and pick it up later. I told Louie that until then, he could play with my favorite stuffed giraffe.

Soon everyone was crammed into the kitchen as my mom and grandmother prepared a pancake breakfast for the massive crew. Mr. Marcus had been on the phone trying to reach his insurance agent to find out what to do next, but he could not reach him. Feeling frustrated, he sat at the table and dug into the pancakes. Everyone else ate like they were starving. Butter and syrup were in danger of running out, but it was clear that my mom and grandmother were enjoying taking care of the displaced family.

Mr. and Mrs. Marcus were really nice people, and they continually thanked my family for allowing them to spend the night, as all of their relatives lived out of state. I had always found the twins, Louie and Teddy, adorable, but I hadn't known how much noise three-year-olds can make nor what messes they could make in less than thirty seconds. They screamed when they were excited or upset or happy, and after a while I started to become annoyed.

I had to babysit them alone for two hours that day, and they drove me crazy. First they wanted to color, but by the time I took out the crayons and paper, they had changed their minds and wanted to watch TV. After watching for three minutes, they wanted to play with their toys. They did that for five minutes, and then started to whine because they wanted to go outside and play soccer. After the first hour, I was completely exhausted. I dealt with it, though, because I knew it was the right thing to do, and it was only temporary. Although I was only twelve, after having them around for an entire day, I wondered if I would ever have the energy or patience to have kids of my own.

Imagine my surprise when I found out that the Marcuses' home insurance policy would not pay for them to stay in a hotel while their house was being repaired. My kindhearted mother insisted that they stay with us for the two weeks it would take for the repairs to be completed.

Mom was quite calm about her decision to ask them to stay, and so was Grandma. My brothers didn't seem to mind, either, probably because they were gone most of the day working their summer jobs. I, on the other hand, was trying to hide my distress, but my mom, like the trained professional she was, recognized my feelings immediately.

154 KINDNESS AND COMPASSION

She asked me to come upstairs and help her get some spare towels for our guests. We pulled the towels out of the linen closet, then she took me by the hand and brought me into her room to have a chat.

"Angelina, I know that having another family in the house is inconvenient. You won't be able to have the same level of privacy or comfort that you are accustomed to having, and I know how challenging it can be to have two small children in the house. Making such sacrifices to help others in their time of need is the right thing to do, though. This will just be a little test of your patience."

Deep down I knew my mom was right, so I nodded and said, "I'll be patient, Mom, don't worry." She gave me a hug and said, "I know you will do your best. Just remember, patience is like a muscle; the more you use it, the more it develops."

Over the following two weeks, my patience muscles grew to the size of a superhero's. I became accustomed to sleeping on the floor of my mom's room and being woken up every morning at six o'clock by the clamor the twins made. I wasn't bothered by having to wash the extra dishes or waiting a longer time to use the shower. I learned to stay calm when I had to clean up the accidental spills and the stepped-on crayons. I also watched more cartoons than I had in years. But Louie and Teddy also made me laugh all the time with the cute way they mispronounced words like "pasgetti" and "hangerber," and with the funny way they danced when their favorite show was on TV.

When the two weeks were up, they handed me a special drawing they had made for me, hugged me, and told me they loved me. I squeezed them tightly, told them I loved them too, and proudly put their drawing on the refrigerator for everyone to see. I couldn't believe how I had grown to adore these two.

The morning after the Marcus family moved back to their home, I woke up in my own room to total silence. There was no mess on the floor, no wait for the bathroom, no cartoons playing on the TV, and no toys or crayons anywhere to be found. Life had gone back to normal, but it felt so odd. As I sat peacefully eating my cereal, I realized that I was missing Louie and Teddy, their noise, their mess, and their laughter. My observant mother recognized my mood and knew immediately what I was feeling.

"It feels strange not to have Louie and Teddy here now, doesn't it?" she asked.

"Mom," I replied, "it's really quiet now, and I like not having to wake up super early, and I enjoy having my bed back and not having to constantly clean up toys or food from the floor, but . . ."

She smiled and said, "But you miss them. I knew you would, but if I told you that two weeks ago, you wouldn't have believed me."

"How did you know?" I asked.

"Well, I do have three children of my own, and I know how much patience is required day to day to raise very young kids. Over time, what once seemed difficult or impossible to endure becomes easier, even routine. Like a muscle, your patience grows, but along with it, so does your heart." In that moment, I was reminded of how blessed I was to have a mother whose wisdom was surpassed only by her loving heart.

Later that day, I went to see the Marcus family in their home. Louie and Teddy were so happy to see me that they jumped on me as soon as I walked in the door, and I was happy to see them, as well. In fact, I began to visit them every day and became their official babysitter.

The way I see it, they helped me grow my patience muscles so much so that by the time I have kids of my own, not only will I have a massive amount of patience, but I'll have an enormous heart to match.

Helpful Vocabulary Words and Discussion Questions for "A Double Test of Patience"

Vocabulary words: clamor, whine, afford, luxury, frigid, advantage, ablaze, malfunction, appliance, ordinary, circumstances, generosity, crammed, massive, linen, mispronounce, wisdom, adorable, insurance, evacuate

Discussion Questions

1. Why was it so challenging for Angelina to have the Marcus family living in her home?

2. What did she learn from the experience?

3. Have you ever been through an experience that tested your patience? How did you deal with it? What did you learn?

PART VIII

The True Meaning of Love

STORY 21
Love Is a Way to Live

The summer I was twelve, my family and I visited Greece and stayed with my grandparents at their vacation home. I really enjoyed spending so much time with them, because during the school year, between my studies and swimming practice three times a week, I usually visited them only on the weekends. But that summer I was with them every day, and I loved it. Grandpa and I would go for walks by the mountainside, where he would pick fresh figs for us. He showed me the house in the village where he lived as a young boy before he moved to the United States, and told me lots of stories about his family and the way they lived back then.

"Petro, we didn't have any toys to play with; we didn't own a television, a radio, or even a phone. We were very poor, but our lives were rich with love," said Grandpa.

I asked, "What do you mean 'rich in love,' Grandpa? Love is a feeling."

He told me, "Petro, love is not simply a feeling; it is a way to live. When I was a young boy, every morning my mother would make us all breakfast to start our day. Today, when I get up, your grandmother always gives me a cup of her fresh-brewed coffee. That's living in love.

"At night, despite being completely exhausted from working the fields, my father used to tell us stories before we went to sleep, and then kissed us goodnight. When your mom and uncle were younger, I did the same thing. That's living in love.

"If one of my siblings was given a special treat from somebody, like a piece of chocolate or a pastry, rather than eat it immediately, they would bring it home so we could all share it. That's living in love.

"Love is shown in the way you treat other people—and not just your family and friends, but all people. Hugs, kisses, valentines, and gifts are nice, but showing consideration and respect to others, being thoughtful and helpful, that's when you are really living in love. Sometimes you may have to make some difficult decisions or make sacrifices to help meet the needs of others. But know that whatever you give in love is returned to you tenfold."

I had never thought of it that way, but after thinking about what he said, I began to notice examples everywhere of people living a life of love. I saw it when my grandmother came to remind my grandfather that his favorite TV show was about to start when he had forgotten about it. I noticed it when my aunt baked my favorite dessert just because I loved it.

Then I began to recall times in my past when people showed me what love really meant, like all the times my parents would come to my swimming meets just to cheer me on, no matter how hectic their work schedules were. I remembered a time when I got chicken pox and my best friend, Junior, came to visit me instead of going to the movies with others. Grandpa was right when he said love is a way to live.

I made the conscious decision not only to become more aware of people living in love, but to begin showing love to as many people as possible. I started to live love in small ways at first. I volunteered to help my grandparents in the garden by cleaning up the weeds. I helped an older lady from Grandpa's village by carrying her groceries to her home. I volunteered to babysit my neighbor's child one afternoon so she could go to the supermarket. The more I did, the more awesome I felt. What I had not yet realized was that living this way not only gave me more joy and personal fulfillment but was ultimately going to reward me with one of the greatest and most beautiful blessings.

There was no way I could have anticipated the events that would unfold that particular summer day or the effects it would have on my life. The day began like so many others. Grandma and Mom were sitting in the kitchen having a coffee, Grandpa was walking into the kitchen with some freshly picked figs, and Dad was on his laptop, checking his email. I asked my parents if I could go souvenir shopping that afternoon, as our trip was coming to an end, and they agreed. I headed into town by bus and went to the souvenir shops by the pier.

After shopping, I stopped to have lunch before returning home. As I sat down to eat my sandwich, I observed an elderly man with a cane walking on the cobblestone walkway by the water. All of a sudden, he lost his balance and fell into the water. I couldn't believe my eyes, and what was worse, I don't think anyone else had seen it. I got the waiter's attention, told him to call for help, and then ran across the street. At that moment, my grandfather's words came into my head—love is a way to live, it's making difficult decisions and making sacrifices to meet the needs of others—and I made the sudden decision to jump into the water.

The water was very cold, and there were sailboats and rowboats all around. I couldn't see the man anywhere, so I dove under the water to look for him. I was so nervous and scared. Although I was on the swim team, I wasn't trained as a lifeguard, and the water below the pier was nothing like the pool where I practiced and competed. There were no other people in sight, the water was not

clear, and I was frightened of hitting my head against one of the boats when I came up for air, but I chose to keep looking.

After saying a little prayer, I suddenly felt newfound strength. I heard a voice inside me say, "Don't be afraid," and I felt assured that all would be well. Finally, I spotted the man and saw that his jacket was caught on part of a boat, and he couldn't get free. I wasn't sure how much longer I could hold my breath, but I struggled and finally unhooked his jacket and began pulling him toward the surface.

As we pierced our heads through the surface of the water, I saw that help had arrived. Two men pulled the man out of the water and another extended his arm to help get me out. An ambulance arrived shortly after and rushed the man to the hospital while the police and local store owners helped me. One of the store owners brought me some beach towels to dry off with, and another brought me some hot tea while the police contacted my family. They asked me if I wanted to go to the hospital to be examined, but I assured them I was fine; I was more concerned about the man.

A few minutes later, I was elated to see my parents and grandparents arrive. A small crowd of people had assembled around us, and as my parents hugged me, people told them what had happened. My family was delighted that I was safe, and told me how proud they were of my brave efforts. After I rested for a while, we went home so I could change out of my wet clothes and have a warm meal.

I asked my family if we could head to the hospital, because I wanted to check on the man's condition, so my parents, my grandfather, and I headed out as soon as we finished dinner. While we were sitting in the hospital waiting area, I began telling my dad and grandfather more details about my experience that day. My grandfather smiled at me and said, "Petro, today you demonstrated how to live love, and you showed its meaning to others."

Fortunately, the man recovered and was released a few days later. My family and I visited him at his home and met his entire family. A friendship developed between our families, and we would visit them whenever we went to Greece. It was during one such summer that I met and fell in love with his granddaughter, Markella, and today, our families are gathered together to celebrate our wedding. One small good deed, one decision to live love so many years ago, had brought the greatest blessing into my life. Grandpa was right: whatever we give in love is returned to us tenfold. Someday in the future, Markella and I hope to teach this to our own children.

Helpful Vocabulary Words and Discussion Questions for "Love Is a Way to Live"

Vocabulary words: extended, brew, elated, tenfold, pierce, hectic, cobblestone, souvenir, lifeguard, elderly, pier, assure, unhook, surface, demonstrate, delighted, assemble, unfold, observe, particular, sibling

Discussion Questions

1. When Petro first learned about living in love from his grandfather, he began to recognize moments when he had been shown love through the actions of others as examples of living in love. Can you share a memory of when someone exhibited their love to you?

2. What were some of the effects of Petro's heroic actions?

3. What are some of the ways that you show your love to others?

STORY 22
There's Always Room for More

It was almost Christmas, and while Rebecca was excited about all the fun that comes with the holiday, there was a part of her heart that hurt a little. It had been five years since her mom had passed away, and while the family kept up with all their traditions, she and her father always missed her so much more during this time.

As Rebecca and her father were decorating the tree one Saturday morning, she looked at the ornaments and recalled memories of time she spent with her mom shopping for some of them. She shared these stories with her dad, and while the treasured memories made them laugh and smile, there was still a sense of longing in their hearts, knowing that those days would never come again.

As they looked at the completed tree, Rebecca took hold of her dad's hand and exclaimed, "It's perfect! We make a great team." He smiled and agreed, but Rebecca sensed that he had something on his mind. She was right, as he then said he wanted to ask her something.

"Rebecca, I found out that Rose and her husband are coming to Brooklyn to visit with their family and friends. She told me she can't wait to see us, and to see how much you have grown since her last visit. When she received your school picture last month, she couldn't believe her eyes. I would like to invite them to join us for Christmas dinner. I wanted to ask what you thought about the idea."

Rebecca was thrilled. Rose had been one of her mom's best friends. She had moved from Brooklyn to Boston after she married three years earlier. Because of the distance between the two cities, Rebecca and Rose saw each other only once or twice a year, but they often spoke on the phone. Rebecca loved spending time with Rose and listening to stories about the adventures her mom and she had shared.

"Dad, I think that's a great idea. I bet Grandma and Grandpa will be excited to see her, too. Now I'm even more excited for Christmas to come."

On Christmas, the house was filled with the aromas of the glazed ham, roasted potatoes, and Grandma's lasagna. Rebecca helped set the dinner table and had her favorite Christmas carols playing throughout the house to help set the mood. The telephone rang, and she ran to answer it, as the adults had their hands full.

It was Rose, calling with a quick question. She asked if she could bring a guest to dinner. Her sister, Lily, who had recently moved back home to Brooklyn, had had her plans for the evening cancelled. Rose was wondering if the family would mind if she brought Lily along.

Rebecca answered, "Of course not. Like my mom always said, there's always room for more." Rose wanted to speak to Rebecca's father just to make sure, though. He agreed with his daughter and told Rose to bring her sister with her.

A little while later, Rose, her husband, Tyler, and Lily arrived. No one in the family had ever met Lily before, as she had been living and working in Florida after going there for college. She had only been back in Brooklyn for two months and was still adjusting to her new job and the cooler temperatures.

Lily also had known Rebecca's mom. She told stories of how she would follow Rose and her friend throughout the house and never give them any privacy. "When I was little, I wanted to be just like them. When they were fifteen, I took their lip glosses and hid them in my jewelry box. I was only nine, so my parents wouldn't let me have any of my own because I was too young. Rose eventually found out and told on me. My parents weren't very pleased, but for a short while, I felt that I was as glamorous as they were," she said, giggling. Lily was fun and sweet, and everyone immediately felt as if she had always been part of the family.

Rebecca's family kidded the two sisters about being named after flowers. The resemblance between them was strong, especially when they smiled, but Lily's hair and eyes were a bit darker than Rose's.

They had a wonderful time together, and nobody wanted the night to end. To extend the festivities, Rose and Lily invited Rebecca and her family to spend New Year's Eve with them at Lily's new place, and they graciously accepted.

Rebecca could hardly wait for the week to pass, and New Year's Eve finally arrived. At the party, Rebecca couldn't help but notice the amazing framed photographs throughout Lily's home. She learned that Lily had actually taken them herself and that, although Lily was not a professional photographer, she had studied photography in college and continued her beloved hobby.

"Your photographs are amazing! I really love taking pictures, as well. Do you think you could give me a few pointers someday?" asked Rebecca.

"Absolutely, I'd love to," replied Lily.

Sure enough, the two of them met up that weekend, cameras in hand, and headed toward the park. They had a lovely time taking photos of the snow-covered trees and chatting for hours. They went back to Rebecca's house afterward, and her dad insisted that Lily join them for dinner. At the end of the evening, Lily and Rebecca discussed when and where they could meet for their next photography lesson.

A few days later, Rebecca's father said that he had bumped into Lily at the supermarket, and they had had coffee together. He told Rebecca that Lily mentioned she would call her later that week with a few ideas about their next photography adventure. Rebecca was thrilled and full of anticipation—until she heard what her dad said next.

"Sweetheart, I asked Lily to go out to dinner with me this Friday, and she agreed. Are you comfortable with the idea of the two of us going out on a date?"

Rebecca didn't know how to answer. She really liked Lily and got along well with her, but she couldn't help but think of her mom. She blurted out, "It's fine, Dad. She's really nice," but inside she felt conflicted.

That night, as Rebecca lay in bed, she wrestled with her thoughts. She wanted her father to be happy, as she had seen how heartbroken he was after her mom died. For the longest time it seemed that he barely ever smiled. Lily was fun, smart, and easy to get along with, and she adored her, so why was the idea of her dad and Lily getting together uncomfortable for her? Was Lily going to take her mother's place? Would her mom have felt upset about it? All these confusing thoughts were running through her head, but her exhaustion finally overcame her conflicted emotions, and she fell asleep.

The next day, Rebecca went through her typical routine: she went to school, stayed after for choir practice, and then waited for her dad to pick her up. She hadn't thought much about her dad's upcoming date with Lily, as she was distracted most of the day and had pushed it out of her mind. Her dad, though, noticed that she was quieter than usual but didn't press her about it.

Just as they finished dinner, the phone rang; it was Lily calling to make plans with Rebecca for their next photography outing. She had learned about a winter festival a nearby school was hosting and thought it would be a great place to take some photos. Rebecca had heard about the festival and really wanted to go. She hated that she now felt awkward talking to Lily, because she really adored her. While her initial reaction was to say yes, she told Lily that she wasn't sure if she could make it. She lied and said that her friend might be having a birthday party that day. Lily told her not to worry and that they could get together some other time, but Rebecca felt awful about lying to her.

The next day Rose came by to say goodbye to Rebecca before going back to Boston. "I passed by your father's office to say goodbye to him, but saying goodbye to you, Rebecca, is always so much harder for me." Rose took a long look at her, smiled, and said, "Every time I see you, you look more and more like your mom. I miss her like crazy, but seeing you makes me feel like she's still here."

"Rose, thank you for saying that. I miss her so much, too, and I don't want her to be forgotten."

"Sweetheart," Rose asked, "what makes you think that your mom could ever be forgotten?"

With tears suddenly streaming from her eyes, Rebecca blurted out, "Well, what happens if someday my dad gets remarried and his new wife doesn't want him to remember my mom?"

Rose tenderly hugged Rebecca and said, "I think I know what this is about. You're feeling nervous about your dad going out with Lily, aren't you? My sweet girl, we don't know what the future holds for those two, or if someday your dad will get married to another woman. But what I do know is that even if your father has a new wife some day, he will not forget your mother. They loved each other so much, and that love doesn't disappear or fade even when one of them dies."

"Rose, I really like Lily; in fact, I think she's pretty awesome. I can totally understand why my dad would like her. But as soon as I found out he asked her on a date, I felt guilty about liking her, like I was betraying my mom."

"Let me explain this in a different way so that you understand it better," said Rose. "When you were in elementary school, you used to spend every day with your friend Sari, but then she moved, and you both went to different middle schools. At your new school, you met Andrea and soon became friends. When you became friends with Andrea, did you suddenly stop caring for or loving Sari?"

"No, of course not," Rebecca answered. "I still love Sari, even if we don't see each other as often. I understand your point, Rose. You don't stop loving one person just because a new person comes into your life."

"The heart can expand immeasurably, sweetheart, like a huge balloon that can stretch bigger and bigger yet never pop. No one gets pushed out when somebody else comes in. The heart expands and stretches to fit more. No one gets replaced, so there is no reason to feel guilty about loving another person. There's always room for more."

Rebecca smiled, because Rose's words sounded just like something her mom would say. "Thanks, Rose. I feel better already."

The two of them said their goodbyes, and Rose went on her way back home. A few hours later, Rebecca called Lily and told her that she would be able to go to the festival with her after all.

While Rebecca didn't know what the future held for her, her dad, and Lily, she decided that she would just allow her heart to be open to the possibility of loving more. Because as her mom always said, "There is always room for more."

Helpful Vocabulary Words and Discussion Questions for "There's Always Room for More"

Vocabulary words: longing, aroma, glazed, resemblance, blurt, photography, wrestle, conflicted, adore, fade, distract, choir, immeasurable, tenderly, pointers, glamorous, cancel, streaming, typical, traditions

Discussion Questions

1. Why did Rebecca feel guilty about caring for Lily after her father asked Lily on a date?

2. How was Rebecca helped by Rose's explanation of how the heart has room to love many people?

3. New people come into our lives through birth, marriage, and new experiences. Have you ever felt conflicted about letting a new person into your heart?

Story Directory

Below is a list of the stories found in this book. Each story is briefly summarized, followed by notes that describe the subject matters addressed in that story. Please use the Story Directory as a reference tool and a guide to help you find specific topics for reading or discussion.

1. *The Light Giver*: Mike, a building contractor, always seems to know what people need to hear. He helps a writer clear his writer's block by teaching him to help others when he can't help himself.

    Topics addressed: dealing with pressure you put on yourself, helping others when you can't help yourself

2. *Gabriel's Journey:* Young Gabriel, wheelchair-bound after a car accident, is battling the challenges and pain of physical therapy. His demeanor and outlook are changed after he has a chance encounter with another patient.

    Topics addressed: facing challenges and discouragement, gaining a new perspective

3. *The Messenger*: A town is baffled when anonymous messages mysteriously pop up on people's doorsteps with the perfect advice for each recipient. As a reporter tries to solve the mystery of who the messages are from, more and more citizens take the initiative

to send additional messages to help and encourage others.

Topics addressed: encouraging others, spreading goodwill anonymously

4. *The Most Beautiful Girl in the World*: Erica's self-confidence is crushed when her classmates begin to tease her. She learns over time that their hurtful words do not define her, and eventually becomes a teacher who instructs her students about the power of their words.

Topics addressed: bullying, the power of words, self-acceptance, releasing negativity

5. *It's Your Choice*: Debbie learns from her grandmother that she has a choice about whether or not she allows a bully's words to affect her.

Topics addressed: bullying, taking control of how things affect you

6. *The Big, Ugly, Heavy Suitcase*: Mr. Cycle carries around a suitcase filled with bad memories and previous hurts that prevent him from moving forward in his life. Three young boys help him see that he doesn't have to hold on to his "baggage" anymore.

Topics addressed: setting yourself free of negativity and hurtful experiences

7. *The Race*: Jackie is a runner who desperately wants to win the big race but is always coming in second to Mary. When she has the opportunity to prevent her competition from showing up, she decides to take it. After she wins the race, she is ridden with guilt and regret.

Topics addressed: listening to your conscience, dealing with guilt and regret

8. *The Guilt Bugs*: When Jamie breaks her sister's trophy and tries to hide the truth by lying, her conscience leads her to have a nightmare where she is swarmed by the "guilt bugs."

Topics addressed: lying, how guilt affects you, relief after confessing the truth

9. *The What-If Monster*: After moving to a new town, Eva is distressed by frightening "what-if" questions regarding this new chapter in her life. With the help of her great-aunt Millie, she learns that most of the things the what-if monster tries to scare us about never happen, and that she can replace the scary questions with positive ones.

    Topics addressed: fear of the unknown, fear of new experiences

10. *Do It Afraid*: Jennifer is afraid to admit to her friends that she doesn't enjoy the musical group that they love. When the group is coming to town for a concert, she even considers canceling plans with her dad to go to a baseball game, which she has been looking forward to, in order to attend the concert with her friends. Jennifer finally finds the courage to be honest with her friends and finds true acceptance.

    Topics addressed: facing the fear of rejection, wanting acceptance from peers

11. *The Truth Behind Their Words:* Best friends Alex and John face a crisis in their friendship when it is strained after John starts spending more time with his teammates on the basketball team. Each boy thinks he is losing his best friend. Alex's uncle encourages him to talk to John, and the boys resolve the misunderstanding.

    Topics addressed: the fear of being replaced by another, the secret pain hidden in words

12. *Let Your Light Shine*: Peter is an extremely bright boy who always excelled academically. When some of his fellow classmates tease him about his grades, he decides he doesn't want to be different and stops trying his best. When his hero, famous baseball player Zach Madden, speaks at his school, Peter learns that he should always be the best version of himself.

    Topics addressed: being your personal best, not being afraid to stand out from your peers

13. *Not Like Everybody Else*: Patti begins to feel insecure about her fashion sense when everyone at school is wearing the same look and no one compliments her on her new outfit. Her mother

designs something special for her, which helps her realize that it is better to be an original than to be just like everybody else.

Topics addressed: being unique, not comparing yourself to others

14. *A Person of Excellence*: Antonia's parents had taught her to be a person of excellence. When she decides to run in an election for school representative, she is given some negative information about one of her running mates. She has to decide whether or not she will expose the negative information to guarantee her win.

    Topics addressed: being a person of integrity, being your personal best

15. *Eleni's Disappointment*: When Eleni's grandmother falls and requires surgery, Eleni and her mom need to cancel their vacation plans. She learns that making sacrifices to help others often brings surprising rewards.

    Topics addressed: handling disappointment, honoring family responsibilities, the rewards of doing the right thing

16. *Tommy's Bike*: After his bike is stolen due to his carelessness, Tommy works for two years to save up enough money to buy a new one. When the bike gets vandalized by a jealous classmate, Tommy learns to practice forgiveness and shows the vandal kindness.

    Topics addressed: envy, forgiveness, goal setting, having appreciation for things.

17. *Tuning In to Your Truth*: Charlie's school band is competing with the band from his former school. When his current bandmates criticize the other school's band and students, Charlie is torn about admitting that the other students are his friends. With the help of his uncle and his band teacher, Charlie finally shares the truth with his classmates.

    Topics addressed: preconceived judgments, honoring truth and friendship, wanting to be accepted by peers

18. *Penny's Surprise*: After Penny witnesses the effect her mother's kindness has on a certain man's demeanor, she decides to spread kindness to others and sees firsthand how it returns to her.

Topics addressed: showing kindness and having it returned to you

19. *A Trip to the Senior Home*: Ms. Brooks's class visits a senior home and is touched by the impact they have on the seniors and themselves. They learn that good deeds bring great rewards.

    Topics addressed: respect, appreciation, kindness to elders

20. *A Double Test of Patience*: After a neighbor's house catches fire, Angelina and her family open their home to the neighbors and their young twins. Although the now-crowded home is chaotic and requires everyone to have a great deal of patience, once the neighbors move back home, Angelina ends up missing the chaos.

    Topics addressed: patience and its rewards, making sacrifices to help others, generosity to those in need

21. *Love Is a Way to Live*: When Petro's grandfather teaches him that love is shown by one's actions, he decides to show love to others around him. When an elderly man falls off a pier, Petro saves his life and is eventually rewarded with the greatest love of his life.

    Topics addressed: love is shown by the way you treat and serve others, showing love has great rewards

22. *There's Always Room for More*: Rebecca and her widowed father are visited by her late mom's best friend, Rose, and Rose's sister, Lily. While Rebecca really likes Lily, she feels guilty about it, especially after her father expresses a romantic interest in Lily. Over time, Rebecca learns that no love is replaceable and that the heart always has room for more.

    Topics addressed: opening your heart to new people and experiences after a loss without feeling guilty, the heart always has the potential to fit more love

About the Author

PEGGY D. SIDERATOS is a seasoned elementary school teacher who received her Bachelor of Arts and graduated Suma Cum Laude with a Master of Science in Bilingual Elementary Education from Brooklyn College. She worked for a parochial school in Brooklyn for several years and later served on their school board. Peggy also taught for the New York City Department of Education at PS/IS 180 in Brooklyn for ten years, where she was part of the Gifted and Talented program. She has experience with a variety of grades and taught students from Kindergarten through Grade 7. Her love and devotion to children are the motivating forces for writing these books.

During her years of teaching she organized several food, clothing and toy drives for the homeless and took her students on many trips to senior citizen homes and centers in an effort to instill in them the value of community service. Along with her students, she also created several class newspapers that were sold school-wide to raise money for charities.

Peggy is also an active member of the Dafnonas Society, a not-for-profit organization that raises money for charities and individuals who need help. She has served as their youth coordinator for the past six years and has worked with the children to donate thousands of dollars to the Make a Wish Foundation, St Jude's Children's Hospital, Shriners Hospital for Children, and the Ronald McDonald House.

Her ultimate dream is for all children to grow up with a greater sense of confidence, inner peace and with a heart filled with compassion, empathy and kindness for themselves and others.

To learn more about Peggy and her books, visit www.thelightgiverstories.com.